ART LINKLETTER

The New
Kids Say
the Darndest
Things!

Illustrated by CHARLES M. SCHULZ

Introduction by WALT DISNEY

Dale/Caroline
Dale Books
New York

To the children of the world—I love you.

Contents

Foreword

WHY am I writing another book about kids? Several reasons. The first one, probably, is that wherever I travel on my lecture tours and personal appearances, people say "when are you going to give us some more laughs with the kids?" And the sad truth is that we DO need something to laugh about these days—because the happy sound of laughter is being drowned out by the cries of rage and frustration coming from too many people who are mad, sad, lonely, rebellious, frustrated, depressed, frightened, or freaked out.

Another reason for the book is that kids have brought so much pleasure into my life that I like to share it. And as you read these pages, I hope I'll be sharing it with you. After twenty-five years of interviewing little ones on my *House Party* over CBS, five days a week, fifty-two weeks a year . . . and after working with children through the YMCA, the Boy Scouts, the 4H Clubs, Foster Parent Plans, and raising my own little Links, I have concluded that kids give us the most refreshing humor of all.

This book is a mixture of old and new. I have included the best from my first KIDS SAY book, added some brand new sparklers from recent interviews, sprinkled in some gaspers told me by parents, teachers, and youth leaders, and then updated the whole thing with some of my own thoughts about this "electric generation" which has been so changed by the six-hours-a-day schedule of TV watching that has become the average in the U.S. over the last ten years.

Kids today have a surprisingly large vocabulary picked up from commercials, news broadcasts, and the general run of shows they are generally watching in a sadly unsupervised way. Their "skim" knowledge of the universe might lead you to believe that they are much more sophisticated, wise, and mature in their approach to life. But a small "scratch" (verbally speaking) beneath that covering reveals the same wonderful, ignorant, curious, uncomprehending view of life.

For instance, I asked a seven year old girl what she wanted to be when she grew up and she instantly spouted "gloriously liberated!" Somewhat taken aback by this unexpectedly literate answer, I gasped "where did you hear that?" And she nonchalantly said "Oh, in a TV commercial where they're selling *autonomical* dishwashers. Whatever that is."

Another five year old who had apparently been weaned on a steady diet of news broadcasts had a different answer to this same question "what do you want to be when you grow up?" "*Alive!*"

Kids not only *say* the darndest things, they sometimes *pray* the darndest things. Like the little boy who patterned his prayer on what he thought he heard in church. "And forgive us our trashbaskets," he prayed fervently, "as we forgive those who put trash in our baskets."

Here's hoping the following stories don't end up as trash in your basket. If they do, I'll never forgive myself. Or you!

ART LINKLETTER
January, 1978

Introduction

WITH this collection of funny and oddly wise sayings of small boys and girls, Art Linkletter makes a priceless contribution to the anecdotal literature of childhood.

I know of no one else who could have done it so delightfully and with such insight into bright young minds and guileless young hearts.

Art himself retains the lively spirit and zest of youth which have made a legion of kids confide in him and regard him as a special friend. I have seen him with his own children, the kids of his neighborhood and the hundreds of young guests he has interviewed on his television show.

The following pages represent the response of thousands of boys and girls to his deft and sympathetic pryings into their beliefs, experiences and reactions to the adult world.

It is a precious record—a treasury of things so close and meaningful to little folk in a big new world and so increasingly remote to most of us as we grow up.

Somewhere among the hundreds of amusing anecdotes in the Linkletter collection every reader is sure to find one that is reminiscent of his own youth or the confidences of his sons or daughters.

Here is the exciting play of fanciful imagination, of lively curiosity, of the need to find out, to seem wise beyond their years. Here is the nonsense that sometimes makes strange sense, the quick inventions, the unconscious witticisms—the wonderful, intimate revelation of childhood in honest, funny, sometimes pathetic sayings about itself.

It is a shame that we must lose this forthright honesty, this searching curiosity, this drive of the imagination toward great deeds, exciting adventure, knowledge, achievements to win fame and honors and pleasure, in the process of "growing up."

These are the qualities which the inventors retain, men like Edison, Fulton, DeForest—artists, poets, musicians, scientists, naturalists. The natural heritage of children.

Age has nothing to do with it; I mean the actual years. It is the conventions, the expected staid behavior of adults, the embarrassment at being thought "childish," which finally cramps down our imaginative flights and inventive curiosity.

I myself have been flattered by the reputation for never having quite grown up . . . Well, if I ever was a potential champ in this respect, I now willingly hand the crown over to Art.

I believe he is on close confidential terms with more youngsters than any other man of our day. He has done us all a fine service in publishing this record of what our children believe and the happy way in which they let us back into their world of wonders and magic—that blessed place and state of being of which a great writer has said: "Heaven lies about us in our infancy."

Walt Disney

Chapter 1

Two for the Show

AFTER MORE than forty years of interviewing people of all ages, under the most informal, unrehearsed conditions (on the street, in restaurants, hotels, ballrooms, maternity wards, marriage license bureaus, on stages, and at expositions) I have concluded that without doubt the most candid, and shocking answers are from two general classes of guests: (1) Women over eighty who have finally shed all hypocrisy and evasiveness and who are prepared to tell their innermost thoughts, and (2) Children under ten who really don't know that they are spilling the beans. They are brightly guileless, straightforward, and their answers are a strange mix of raw truth, garbled impressions, and pure imagination. And the younger they are, the more likely the combination will result in a very short fuse leading to a mirthful bombshell. Occasionally, they are "floating free" to such an extent that they have not really understood *where* they are or *what* they are doing, much less what they are *saying*.

1

Often, after interviewing four tiny tots of four or five years of age, on a full coast to coast network of CBS television stations, I'll feel a small tug at my coat backstage, and a little anxious face looks up at mine and lisps, "Mr. Winkwetter, when does the show begin?"

It was from one of these darlings that I heard the delightful interpretation of "helping Mommy with breakfast." The four year old girl had insisted that she definitely helps her Mother with the morning meal, and when I asked for details, she cheerfully replied: "I put the bread in the toaster. The only trouble is, I can't flush it."

Another pre-schooler assured me solemnly that "We just had a baby at our house. Mama says it's the opposite sex, but I don't know what that is!"

Families fascinate youngsters of all ages, but it might surprise some parents and relatives to know where they are in the pecking order. I asked a five year old boy what kind of a family he had, and he responded alertly: "We have a dog, a fish, a parakeet, then there's my Mother, my Dad, and my Grandfather."

"How old is your Grandfather?" I asked.

"Oh, I don't know," he shrugged his shoulders unconcernedly, "but we've had him for a long, long time."

JUST AS A new born babe is protected from many viruses by his mother's immunity, passed on to him for the first year in some magical way, so are the tiniest tykes shielded from life's frustrations and embarrassments through a heaven-sent security blanket of innocence. If they don't know, they'll guess with no fear of looking silly, and no worry about being logical.

A little girl with dark blonde curls and a blue ribbon in her hair looks very much in earnest as she tells me what she wants to do with the rest of her life:

"I want to be a nurse and fix up sick people."

"What would you do if I came into your office with a broken arm, a broken leg, and a broken neck?"

"I'd cry."

There's a story that's told of a four year old boy who was visiting a farm for the first time and was taken to see the lambs. Finally he worked up enough courage to pat one. "Why," he said delightedly, "they make them out of blankets!"

A school teacher told me of one young applicant for pre-school activities who was asked to take a physical examination before being admitted. The doctor asked him, "Do you have any trouble with your ears or nose?"

"Yes," he replied. "They are always in the way when I take off my pajamas."

One morning on stage at CBS a nursery babe smiles up at me from her tiny chair: "How did your folks meet and fall in love?" I asked her, hoping for something sweet.

"It happened in heaven!"

"In heaven!!" I repeated in surprise. "How?"

"They were babies waiting to be born and God put them on the same pink cloud."

WHAT'S IT like to be four? It's to be like the boy who brought his puppy to visit his grandmother. She was busy fixing dinner and paid no attention to the pup. After a while the boy, his eyes filling with tears, asked her reproachfully,

"Aren't you even going to speak to your granddog?"

Another tiny moppet is waiting to be vaccinated, but she's determined to be brave. All goes well until she is face to face with the needle. Now she leans over and speaks softly into the doctor's ear: "I think your mother is calling you."

I had a typical quartet of five year olds one morning, all scrubbed and shining and fidgety. Three boys, one girl. They wanted to be, from left to right, a doctor, a lion-tamer, a movie star, and a trained nurse.

I asked the future lion-tamer what he'd have to remember if he wanted to succeed with his four-footed friends. "To stay away from their mouths," he promptly replied, which summarized that profession very neatly.

I asked the Cary Grant of the next generation why he wanted to be a movie star, and a blissful expression spread across his face. "I'd like the life," he confided.

"What would that be like?" I asked him cautiously.

"Well," he dreamily went on, "a movie star wakes up about ten and has breakfast in bed. Then he takes a big car to the studio and kisses girls all day. Then he has dinner at some fancy place where a lot of pretty girls smile at him, and if he wants to, he marries the prettiest one late that night!"

I didn't try to disillusion him. I moved hastily on to the future Florence Nightingale.

"So you want to be a nurse," I reminded her. "What would you do if I came to you with a terrible, drippy cold?"

"Nothing," she decided.

"Nothing?" I echoed. "Why not?"

"Because I wouldn't be there. I'd be gone," she said serenely. "Who wants to catch your old cold?"

Then, there was the very young man who wanted to be a cat when he grew up.

"A cat?" I echoed. "What kind of cat?" "A tom-cat," he said promptly.

"Why a tom-cat?" I asked.

"I don't know," he said wistfully, "but that's what my dad says *he'd* like to be!"

FEW THINGS in childhood have the delicious excitement of a genuine secret. The trouble with secrets is that they're *most* fun when they bubble up and pop out, and then they're gone, and you have to go looking for another one.

"What's your favorite game?"

"Hide and seek."

"Why?"

"Because no one can ever find me."

"Where do you hide?"

"I can't tell: it's a secret."

"Come on, you can tell me. I'll never tell anybody."

"All right. It's in the garbage can."

◆ ◆ ◆

"Do you have a secret?" I teased a dimply little blonde girl.

"Yup, but I'm not ever going to tell anybody even if they torture me to death."

"Wow!!" I responded. "That must be the biggest secret in the whole world."

"Well," she hesitated, "really it's not very big."

"What do you mean, not very big?"

"It's my pink pants with the blue bows!" and exploding with laughter, she pulled up her dress to show me her secret underwear.

◆ ◆ ◆

Sometimes I have the feeling that kids are the original source of humor. It just bubbles up from some inner spring, unbidden, refreshing, and unending. Like the four year old boy who had an answer for everything:

"Do you know what a weasel is?"

"Sure. Weasels are things that break out all over your face when you're sick."

"What do you think of the saying, 'the early bird gets the worm'?"

"He's welcome to it. I ate one once and it tasted like cold spaghetti."

"What's the most fun at nursery school?"

"Making castles and animals in the sand pile."

"What's the worst thing about nursery school?"

"Getting the sand out of my pants."

"Really?"

"Sure. If you'll unbutton my pants, I'll show you!"

◆ ◆ ◆

"What would you do if you could be invisible for a day?" I asked some five year olds. When they just stared at me uncomprehending, I realized that they hadn't the faintest idea what "invisible" meant, so I went on to describe how no one could see them but they could act just as they wanted to with no fear of a spanking.

◆ "I'd rob a big bank and buy a toy store," chirped the first.

◆ "I'd marry somebody rich before he knew what was happening," said a redhead.

◆ "I'd change all the clocks to different times and mix everybody up."

◆ "I'd eat my brother's dessert right in front of him, and then my sister's, and then my daddy's

. . ." her voice trailed off, overcome by the delicious imaginary scene.

◆ ◆ ◆

Grown-ups forget the first years when we're all so helpless, small, and at the mercy of a world designed for big people. To the very young, any knowledge whatever is a source of great pride. For example:

"Can you tell your right from your left?"
"No."
"Well, then what *do* you know?"
"I know my front from my back."

◆ ◆ ◆

"Do you have any fun?" I asked a worried little boy. "You don't look happy."

"Well," he said, "I *thought* I was going to have fun at my uncle's farm yesterday, but nothing much happened."

"Surely, something must have happened to make you look so glum."

"Well, yeah, a rooster bit me on the belly button."

◆ ◆ ◆

Three year old Steve was one of the brightest of the really tiny youngsters I've ever had on the air, but his notions about the operation of a modern dairy were delightfully mixed up. After telling me that his parents had taken him on a tour of a dairy, he gave me this version of the expedition:

"There's this big brown cow with the red eyes and wet tongue and he has a balloon under him full of nibbles. The man gets a pail of milk and a fire hose, and they put the fire hose on one of the nibbles and put the other end in the milk pail. Then they turn on this machine and fill up the cow full of milk."

◆　◆　◆

Surest-fire of all questions for all ages has to be the eternal "What do you want to be when you grow up" variety. And the smaller, the better. "You're only four, Margie," I began. "Do you have any idea what you'll grow up to be?"

"Yep," she seemed so positive. "A mother. But I certainly don't want any children."

◆　◆　◆

"What's your ambition, young man?"

"To be a skin diver in the Navy."

"What if you were swimming along and suddenly you saw a man-eating shark?"

"I'd tell him, 'Go find a man; I'm just a little boy.'"

◆　◆　◆

"What do you want to be, Donald?"

"An artist, so I can draw rainbows."

"What's at the end of the rainbow?"

"A plug."

"Where have you been seeing your rainbows?"

"In the bathtub."

◆ ◆ ◆

"What do you want to be?"

"A policeman."

"What's the most important thing to remember to be a good policeman?"

"Don't wet your bed."

◆ ◆ ◆

"What's your ambition?"

"To be a fireman."

"What if you saw a big fat lady in a tall building that's on fire, and she's yelling for help?"

"I'd send her a big fat fireman!"

◆ ◆ ◆

"What do you want to be?"

"A lifeguard."

"Suppose you saw a man drowning, what would you do?"

"Build a raft."

◆ ◆ ◆

"So you want to be a jet pilot and fly those big planes to Hawaii. What would you do if you were flying at 35,000 feet over the Pacific Ocean and you were half way to Honolulu and there was nothing under you anyplace but water, and all four engines stopped?"

"All four?" he was unbelieving in the panic of the moment.

"Yup, all four stopped dead."

"Well," he began to extemporize, "first, I'd tell the passengers to fasten their safety belts."

"Good! Then what would you do?"

"I'd put on my parachute and bail out."

When the roar of laughter subsided, he explained in a tone of hurt dignity:

"I'm coming back. I'm just going for gas!"

Chapter 2

No Coaching, Please!

CHILDREN under ten and women over eighty give the best interviews on the air today for the identical reason: They speak the plain unvarnished truth. They dish it out in no uncertain terms, with heartfelt emotion coloring each phrase.

No concealing, flattering, hypocritical editorializing among the very young and very old! If you don't want the truth—better not ask them! And don't be shocked if it's phrased in primitive terms.

My own favorite interviews are the younger ones, under seven. Each day brings them some new adventure that is met forthrightly, with head-on courage. One young fellow recently announced: "I was six yesterday!" When I asked what he did to celebrate, he proudly recited: "I had ice cream, cake, candy, milk, and threw up."

Each day as I look at my four tiny guests, fidgeting and scratching and picking and kicking, I wonder what amazing peek we'll get into the folklore and philosophy of their tribal world. Every child, of course, is not a fountainhead of amusing remarks. Some of my guests get stage fright, just like any grown-up. Some of them get emotional and choke up with excitement or panic. Others promptly forget who they are, what their parents do and even why they're on the show.

One aimless little boy couldn't be persuaded to tell me anything. Finally, in desperation, I said: "Well, surely you can describe yourself?"

"Well," he faltered, "I'm mostly dependable."

"What do you mean by that?" I encouraged him.

"Nobody can ever depend on where I'll be or what I'll do."

TEACHERS HAVE a variety of ways of selecting my guests from their classrooms. Sometimes they give impromptu programs where they ask questions much like I do on the air. Sometimes the teachers reward the best pupils with an appearance on the program. And sometimes, I suspect, they pick the kiddies they'd most like to have *out* of the room!

Occasionally, I suspect that a wise teacher will select a youngster whose ego needs a booster shot. Perhaps a young fellow is being trampled on by other brothers or sisters, or he is suffering from inferior feelings because of some unfortunate classroom experience. His selection and appearance on my coast to coast television show may be just the "lift" he needs to help him cope with his personal problems. Since sibling warfare is incessant, many a younger brother or sister finally gets a long overdue revenge on the "stay-at-home" who is watching the show in anticipatory dread.

Gregory, aged five, announced to me that he'd like to advertise something on the program. When I inquired about his product, he replied:

"I want to sell my sister for half price. That's fifty cents!"

"What would you do with the money?" I blandly carried on.

"Buy a baby brother that'd be some fun for a change."

"Where would you buy him?"

"From my mother, of course. She's the one who produces them all."

And then there was the boy who wistfully dreamed of being a giraffe. When I asked what was so great about that, he stated:

"Then my sister couldn't slap me in the face without getting a stepladder."

And there are more gems of the same purest ray serene—lots more:

Any brothers or sisters?
   One big brother.
Any problems?
   I can't tell you.
Why not?
   Because he's sitting in the audience.

Have any brothers?
   One, seven years old.
Is he in school today?
   No, he's home playing sick so he can watch me.

◆ ◆ ◆

Any brothers or sisters?
    A brother and two sisters.
How would you describe them?
    My brother's a brat, one of my sisters is a little squirt and one's a monkey.

◆ ◆ ◆

Any brothers or sisters?
    I think I have two brothers.
What are their names?
    I think one is Sandra.
Isn't that a girl's name?
    I guess that isn't his name.
What's the other brother's name?
    I don't know; they never told me.
Are you SURE *you have two brothers?*
    No.
What DO *you have?*
    Three guppies.

◆ ◆ ◆

Any brothers or sisters?
    I have a brother one week old.
What can he do?
    He can say "Mamma" and "Daddy."
Can he walk?
    No, he's too lazy.

◆ ◆ ◆

Any brothers and sisters?
    A two months old brother.

How does he behave?

He cries all night.

Why is that, do you think?

He probably thinks he's missing something on television.

◆　◆　◆

Who talks longest on the phone in your family?

My sister.

What does she talk about?

Mainly who she's going to beat up next, and I'm high on the list.

◆　◆　◆

How old is your brother?

Six.

Does he have any unusual or interesting ways of getting into trouble?

Well, this week he dropped all the guest towels into the toilet and yesterday he gave the goldfish a bubble bath.

HOW CHILDREN are selected to appear on the *House Party* show is the question asked by thousands of letter writers. During holiday weeks, and in the summertime, our "interviewees" come from private schools, YMCA, YWCA, Boy Scout and other club groups. They also are picked from auditions held each month by our own "teacher," as a result of the thousands of letters we get suggesting children for the show.

Most of these letters, of course, come from proud grandparents, with a generous number from mothers and dads. It's often quite a shock for a parent to march proudly into our office with his "brilliant" child in hand, ready for an audition, and then squirm with frustration when the young prodigy stands there wordless and defiant. The boy who never stops talking from morning until night, and who utters pearls of amusing wisdom every time he opens his mouth, becomes a Sphinx. I shudder to think of the mayhem that occurs in the family car on the way home after the debacle.

To avoid such a speechless occasion on the air, I meet with the youngsters for five or ten minutes before each broadcast, so that we can get acquainted and I can find out which ones of the four will be most apt to "open up" with me. Every child reacts differently to different people, and whereas a boy may chatter like a magpie with our teacher, he may be uncomfortable or uneasy with me. My job is to warm up the recalcitrant ones, and encourage the talkative ones to be even more so.

I do this in a variety of ways. I tease them. I promise them extra desserts for being good. And I sometimes have to be stern with them. Some of the kids are so excited they become almost hysterical and have to be quieted down and told that they are being watched by the President himself.

NO CHILD is ever told what to say or what to think before he goes on the air. To begin with, there's no writer in Hollywood capable of producing the original, off-beat remarks that come from a six year old mind, and if we did unearth such an adult genius to write "funny sayings," any "rehearsed" delivery would lose all the spontaneous spark and fun. And, of course, there's one more important detail: we wouldn't have the nerve to cue a child to say some of the startling things that come popping, unbidden, out of his mouth.

Teachers and parents alike watch and listen in fear and trembling when I ask the innocently loaded question: "Do you have any instructions from anyone today?" Here are a few choice samples:

◆ "My mother told me to pay no attention to all the crazy things my Dad told me."

◆ "My mother told me to be sure not to tell what the neighbors are saying about us."

◆ "My mother told me to be sure to show you my new pink pants that tinkle." (They had bells.)

◆ "My Dad told me just one thing: To keep my pants up." (Five year old boy.)

◆ "My mother told me to keep my legs together." (Five year old girl.)

◆ "My teacher told me not to be funny. That's what *you* get paid for."

◆ "My mother told me not to say that the last thing she said was to go to the toilet before I went on the program."

◆ "Nobody told me anything. My Dad was late for work and was gulping down his breakfast. My mother was washing her hair. Grandmother had a stomachache. Everybody was too busy to tell me anything."

◆ "My mother told me to be sure and thank you if you give me a nice present. Are you?"

◆ "My teacher told me that if you asked me to tell you about her, to not say she's very old because she heard a little boy on your program who said: 'What an old teacher!' "

This prompted me to ask him: "How old would you say your teacher is?" "Oh, about ninety!"

SOMETIMES THE parental instructions are a bit more involved. Here are some typical samples:

What did your mother tell you not to say today?
    She told me not to tell you that she works on a couch.
What kind of work does she do on a couch?
    She cleans them, so I don't know what's wrong with that.

◆   ◆   ◆

What did your folks tell you before leaving?

My mother told me no matter what else happened to keep my shirt tail in.

◆ ◆ ◆

Did your mother give you any directions?
Yes, she told me to be sure and tell you what kind of job she has with the county.
What does she do?
The only thing I can remember is that whatever she does it's a long word and I forgot it.

◆ ◆ ◆

Did your parents give you any instructions?
My mother said to be funny and my dad told me to order an expensive steak.

◆ ◆ ◆

My mother told me to be sure not to act off today.
What do you mean "act off"?
That means not to tell any bad jokes.
I wouldn't think you knew any bad jokes.
Sure, I know lots of them. My brother tells them to me, like the one, "Help! I can't swim!" "Why?" "I'm not in the water!"

◆ ◆ ◆

Did your mother tell you anything before coming on the show?
Yes. She told me not to fall asleep.

◆ ◆ ◆

Any order from your mother today?

She told me to not say any bad words.

I bet you don't even know any.

Well, I had some when I started out this morning, but I lost them somewhere.

◆ ◆ ◆

Did your dad tell you anything before coming down here?

He told me to be sure to walk on the outside of the women.

Aren't you liable to wear them out that way?

Oh, I don't mean on the outside of them, themselves. I mean when we walk.

What's the idea behind that custom, do you know?

It's in case the drunk driver jumps the curb, then the first person who'd be killed would be me.

◆ ◆ ◆

Any instructions?

My mom told me *not* to act normal.

◆ ◆ ◆

Did your mother tell you anything not to say?

Yes, not to say shut up to anybody.

When do you ever say that?

To my sister and, when she's not around, to my boy friend.

Why?

Because everybody talks too much except me.

FROM LETTERS, conversations, and via the grapevine of the PTA, I have been able to piece together quite accurately the sequence of events leading up to an average child's appearance on my show. First, there is the breathless announcement by the youngster, himself, that he has been picked by his teacher to be on Art Linkletter's program. The parents look at each other with the happiness that comes from having the world finally learn of their remarkable offspring. All along they knew he'd be President or maybe even a movie star. Now, it is all beginning to come true.

In the first flush of success, there's a mad rush to get off the letters, wires and calls to friends, relatives, neighbors and creditors. The date of the big appearance is circled in red on the calendar, and everyone tells Junior what a fine little fellow he is.

Then, as Mother and Dad begin to "catch" the show and hear the brutal frankness of the revelations, they begin to look at one another guardedly, and the first insidious worry creeps into the happy household. What if Sonny Boy tells about Uncle John's poker sessions? What if the Pride-and-Joy blabs the truth about their credit rating? And, horror of horrors, what if he repeats on the air what Daddy has privately been saying about the Big Boss these past three years!!

The next few weeks in the month before the curtain goes up are busy ones for Junior. Brainwashing is a mild term for what occurs.

He is indoctrinated, coaxed, threatened, and rehearsed. The dirt under the living room carpet is minimized; the sneaky next door neighbor is eulogized; and the long list of relatives is trotted out with shiny new halos adorning each head. Home has become Heaven indeed.

My most effective attack on this defensive position is a fairly sneaky one. I ask one simple question: "What did your Mommy tell you *not* to say?" And what lovely answers we get! Full, complete, and perfectly rehearsed answers . . . rehearsed by Momma, herself.

◆ "My mother told me not to tell any of the family secrets, like the time she dyed her hair blonde and it come out purple."

◆ "My Momma said to keep her condition a big secret. And the funny thing is, I don't even know what a 'secret' is. She just keeps getting fatter and fatter every week."

◆ "My Daddy told me to tell you he worked in a clip joint. Then when you asked me what a clip joint is, I tell you it's a barber shop on Wilshire. Isn't that funny?"

◆ "My Daddy told me not to raise my eyebrows, not to laugh too loud, and no matter where it itches, don't scratch anywhere!"

◆ "My Mother told me not to tell you about my brother, Jimmy." He paused and gulped bravely. "See, Jimmy is a nasty boy who kicks and spits and hits, and besides he was on your show a long time ago and he said he would sell me for a penny. I'd give *him* away for *nothing!*"

THEN THERE ARE the occasional traps diabolically set by cunning parents . . . traps that I fall into because the child who springs them does it so innocently. Listen:

"What's new and exciting around your house?"

"My mother's had more babies in the last week than she's had in six months."

"I . . . *what*?" I gasped. "How many babies did she have last *week*?"

"Eight."

"What's this, some kind of joke?" I protested.

"No. She works in the delivery room of the hospital."

"Aha! Did she tell you to say this to startle me out of my wits?"

"No," the boy calmly revealed, "but my father did."

The teachers come in for their share of attention as a result of what goes on in the selection and occasional "practicing" for the big appearance. The youngsters have rare assurance in their analysis of "why" they are on the show. One boy blandly said:

"The teacher picked me because I'm funny. And irresistible to women."

"How do you know that?"

"Wherever I go they keep looking at me and chasing after me and kissing me."

On another occasion, a bright-eyed little fellow, proud as a peacock, boasted:

"My teacher picked me because she said I was the one she'd most like to have *out* of the class for a few hours."

I SUSPECT THAT many a teacher breathes a sigh of momentary relief when she sees some particular hunk of perpetual motion leaving for a morning session with me. The "buzz-saws" of the class actually make some of my best material with their untrammeled minds and unexpurgated comments. Occasionally, the teacher would like to have him suddenly back in class, at any cost! Here's what I mean:

"I was picked to be here because I always speak out of turn in class."

"I'll bet your parents go to school and have nice long talks with your teacher?"

"Oh, yes, they're always paying her visits. And the teacher is just as nice as pie when they're there, and then when my folks leave, she's just as mean as ever."

One candid lad expressed himself clearly as the spokesman for millions of fidgety kids, school-bound down through the ages, when he said:

"If I could change school any way I wanted to . . . there wouldn't *be* any."

Another one particularized: "If I could change school, I'd get rid of all the teachers."

Still another imaginative young soul volunteered: "I think a better name for our school would be 'Alcatraz.' Nobody *ever* escapes."

How many times have you thought about this while struggling through school:

"The best kind of a teacher is a polite, courteous teacher who isn't too easy and still doesn't give you any hard homework."

"Do you have that kind of a teacher?" I asked.

"Well . . . we can't tell yet. It's only the first week and she's still being nice."

ONE DAY I suggested that teachers, too, enjoy a rest from school and look forward to their occasional vacations. I wondered out loud: Where do you guess teachers go for their Christmas vacation? Up went a little lad's hand like a shot, and out came the answer:

"I *know* where mine went. Las Vegas!"

Even principals come in for their share of the harsh limelight. One seven year old stated succinctly: "If I could change school, the first thing I'd get rid of is the principal."

"Why do you say that?"

"Because we don't need her. All she does is to sit there in the office and answer the phone."

Another one said that he'd been picked because his mother was a good friend of the principal, Mr. Smith. When I asked him how he could be sure of that, he said:

"Oh, boy, you ought to hear him whistle at her when she drives by."

And here are some other choice samples:

Why did the teacher pick you today?
   Because I have the gift of gab.
Does it ever come in handy?
   Sure! It got me out of school today, didn't it?

How were you picked today?
   There were three of us boys picked by the teacher. One of them got nervous, one got self-conscious, and I got to come.

◆ ◆ ◆

Why were you chosen to be on the show today?
   Because my mother tells me I'm the most talented child she knows.

◆ ◆ ◆

Why were you chosen to be on the show?
   My teacher says they need different faces, and I have got a different face.

◆ ◆ ◆

Why were you chosen for the show?
   Because I'm not big and I'm not little, and I'm not smart and I'm not dumb. I guess I'm just average.
Why were you picked?
   Because I don't have a sad smile.

◆ ◆ ◆

How were you picked to come today?
   There were three of us girls picked by the teacher and we all three drew paper slips out of a box and it's lucky for you that I won.
Why?
   Because the other girls have chicken pox.

◆ ◆ ◆

Why were you chosen to come on the show?

Because in our room there's some younger and some older, while I'm sort of in the middle ages.

Why were you chosen?

I can't tell you.

Oh, come on . . . tell me.

I can't—but I'll whisper to you. (*Whispers:*) I'm the teacher's pet!

Chapter 3

The Wild Blue Yonder

ONE of my favorite stories about children concerns the little boy in Sunday School who was busily drawing on the back of his song book. When the teacher asked what he was making, he said: "I'm drawing a picture of God."

"But, Bobby," remonstrated the lady, "nobody knows how God looks."

"They will in a minute when I get this done!" he triumphantly replied.

A child's imagination knows no bounds. He lives in at least two or three worlds, whose existence is but dimly remembered by too many of us. Grown-ups let the harsh realities of our workaday world batter down the fragile suspension bridge to those other, happier places in a child's universe.

This effortless "Peter Pan" flight from reality to unreality is not confusing to a child, but occasionally a grown-up is baffled by the quick transition, and wrongfully labels it a "lie." To a child, the imaginary experience is just as real as a true-life happening.

One day I asked a tiny tot if he had any pets at home.

"Yup!" he calmly announced. "I have a little baby porcupine that sleeps with me every night."

"Now isn't that delightful," I replied without batting an eye. "Tell us all about him." And then as quickly as a district attorney, I shot one question after another. "What's his name?"

"Porky."

"Where did you get him?"

"Downtown at a porcupine shop." He grinned up at me.

"How much did you pay for him?"

"One dollar."

"What do you feed him for lunch?"

"Lunch? Well . . . I think . . ."

"Marshmallows?" I suggested craftily.

"Yup! Marshmallows he loves." The youngster swallowed the bait.

"Aha!" I gloated. "How does he eat them?"

There was an imperceptible pause. Then with a happy smile: "He toasts them on his stickers over a campfire!"

CHILDREN LIKE best to imagine they're grown up and able to do all kinds of things better than anybody else. They still see themselves as small as they really are, but capable of knocking down big men, rescuing grown women, and accomplishing large deeds with careless aplomb.

"I'm six years old and I like to fish and hunt bugs," announced a red-headed boy recently.

"What sort of fishing?" I probed.

"Oh, lobsters, crabs, oysters, hamsters, and whales," he reeled off.

"How do you catch hamsters?"

"Grab him by the shell and turn him upside down."

"And whales?" I gently urged him on.

"You get them in a big net."

"How many you caught so far?"

"None."

"Not even a single whale?" I was incredulous.

"Yeah, but I know where one is hiding."

"Where do you catch bugs?" I changed the subject diplomatically.

"In the backyard."

"What kind of bugs?"

"Snails, butterflies, and big long worms." He wrinkled up his nose.

"How long are those worms?" I asked.

"Oh, about as long as rattlesnakes."

"How many have you caught?"

"None," he replied unconcernedly.

"Then how do you know how long they are?" I cross-questioned.

"My sister saw one once."

Changing the subject again, I said: "What will you be when you grow up?"

"An artist."

"Oh, really?" I gasped. "That's quite a switch. What'll you draw?"

"Bugs!"

"Is that the prettiest thing you can think of to draw?"

"Aw, no!" he scratched his stomach reflectively. "I guess the prettiest thing in the whole world is a lady snail with her shell on."

"Does this conversation make you feel itchy?" I inquired.

"Yes."

"You scratch, I'll leave." And I moved on regretfully.

ANOTHER TIME, a young man with great imagination told me that he was one of the best fishermen in his whole family. He had beaten his father, his grandfather, and a large assortment of champions in catching every kind of whale, shark, porpoise, octopus and trout in the sea. When I asked him for the secret of his success, he confided:

"When you throw in your line, the main thing is don't look *hungry* because if the fish sees you up there making faces and licking your lips, they'll know you want to eat them. But if you just pretend that you're not even interested in what's going on, they think that you just like them and want them to eat what you've thrown in, and they bite it!"

LITTLE GIRLS seem to specialize in problems of internal health. They have a marked disposition to be nurses and mothers, and can imagine all kinds of remedies for personal ailments. Quite often, I ask them about a fancied health problem of my own.

"What would you do for me if my heart stopped?" I asked a Junior Nurse.

"I'd just wiggle you around."

One day a little girl hiccuped as she pronounced her name, and I immediately asked if she knew what caused her trouble.

"Yup, I've got hiccups," she diagnosed. "They're three little bugs who stay in your stomach and when you eat too much they jump up and down they're so mad."

Sometimes a child senses that you're teasing him a trifle too sharply, and ends the game with a devastating answer. One such interview was with a tiny girl who had been patiently answering my questions about what she'd do for measles, mumps, earache and such. Finally I went too far. I said: "What would you do if I stopped breathing?"

"I'd bury you!" she scornfully ended the ordeal.

IF CHILDREN don't always tell the truth—and of course they don't—it isn't because they want to avoid it. Usually, it's because they don't know the truthful answer to a question. But if the question requires reasoning and is not too complicated or completely over their heads, their answers almost invariably show great imagination and considerable logic. Take this question and the sharply logical answer:

"What does the saying, 'A wet blanket,' mean?"

"It's the blanket baby lies on."

A little miss of seven said that, and was delighted at the waves of laughter that greeted her response. A few years later, of course, she would have known better. But even if a similar answer to the question had suggested itself to her then, she wouldn't have said it. She would have been inhibited by the adult attitude that some of the commonplace things are not quite nice.

And consider the directness and logic of this:

"What's a goatee?"

"That's easy—a little goat."

The boy wasn't being facetious; he had heard the word "goatee" before and had concluded it meant a little goat.

Any father who has come home after a rough day at work will appreciate the blunt common sense of a seven year old boy's answer to my question: "What do we mean when we say, 'Man's best friend'?"

"A chair," he replied.

Similarly, any mother who has contemplated the household chores that confront her after breakfast, when father has gone to his office and the children are off to school, will understand and think warmly of a girl of eight who said, in answer to this question: "What do you think your mother wants most?"

"To go back to bed."

The real core of humor lies in the "surprise" element, and children are unconscious masters of this art. They lead you on to a conclusion, and then come up with an answer totally unsuspected. Listen to this interview:

"What is your ambition in life?"

"I'd like to be an artist and draw Marilyn

Monroe and Jane Russell," said the boy.

"Ah-ha! That's a good choice," I admired.

"Yup! They'd fill up the whole page!"

THE SUBJECT OF "What you're going to do when you grow up" is a vast one and filled with endless opportunities for imaginative fun. It is perhaps the greatest single daydream of the small fry. And their untrammeled imaginations do things to ordinary jobs that would curl your hair.

"I want to be a boom bomber when I grow up," bravely stated a six year old.

"Never heard of one of those," I gravely replied. "What do they do?"

"Why, that's a guy who goes up in the air, catches eagles by the tail and brings them down for his mommy to cook."

Another earnest youngster came up with the answer to the lament of ministers whose congregations lack the right note of religious conviction:

"I want to be a missionary," he said. "And preach in Africa."

"That's difficult work," I cautioned. "Why did you pick Africa?"

" 'Cause they have big crocodiles down there and if the people don't listen to me I can sic the crocodiles on them!"

This bloodthirsty theme runs through the mind of many a mild-mannered darling. It would frighten you to know how often the curly blonde locks of a little princess cover a head filled with mayhem. This comes out most often when I ask the youngsters what animal they'd like to be and why. Here are a few answers at random from the dear little angels:

◆ "I want to be a lion so I could eat up our landlady."

◆ "I want to be a snake so I could poison our teacher."

◆ "I'd like to be an octopus, so I could grab all the bad boys and bad girls in my room and spank them with my testiticles."

I interrupted this remark hastily with the scientific information: "An octopus has eight *tentacles*, Johnny, and he . . ." "Mr. Linkletter," he broke in, clutching my arm impatiently, "you've got that all wrong. Not *tentacles, testiticles* . . ."

And three minutes later, when the roar of laughter died down, we proceeded with the show . . . not sadder, certainly, but wiser in the ways of a young man's mind.

ONE OVER-ANXIOUS young adventurer revealed how far short the Western movies had fallen in fulfilling the daydream needs of our younger generation when he told me that he was eager to be a real Indian when he grew up. To my question of "Why?" he calmly spelled out his plan of action:

"I want to hide in the bushes, catch cowboys and then kill them."

"For goodness sake," I remonstrated. "Why *kill* them?"

"So I can cook and eat them!" he replied with unruffled demeanor.

A similar case arose in the instance of a future policeman. He had stoutly maintained that he'd be the "best cop anyone ever saw."

"What would you do to be so great?" I probed.

"I'd catch all the criminals in the world and put them in jail for the rest of their life, and then poison them and shoot them!" he said with conviction.

Along this same subject, I was startled one day to find *myself* in the daydream. A youngster had told me he was going to be a famous detective and arrest bad men. I stopped him for a moment with the puzzler: "How would you *know* a bad man? What does a bad man *look* like?" He fixed me with a searching look and began:

"He's a big blond man with blue eyes, wearing a dark suit and a red tie . . ."

"Stop!" I yelled. "You're describing *me*."

BY THE AGE of eleven, sometimes even sooner, children usually come to regard the truth more or less as adults do. That is, they avoid it. They take it apart, and put it back together again as something quite different. This, they know, will please those curious creatures, their elders, who are forever doing the same thing—as they have observed.

For example, when I once asked a boy of

seven how he would go about settling an argument with another boy, he answered promptly, "I'd count to ten, then hit him on the nose." Several years later he would have said no such thing. By that time he would have been so confused and conditioned by his elders and the grinding pressure to conform and be a "nice boy," that he would have said what he knew was expected of him, that is to say, something pious and hypocritical.

Or take the little darling of six, when I asked her what she wanted out of life. She replied brightly, "A rich husband, a Cadillac and twins." When I asked her why she wanted all of those undeniably desirable things at once, she said, with a sort of "what-a-stupid-question" manner:

"To get it all over with at once."

By now she would be terribly embarrassed by such a reply, having probably been thoroughly trained in the usual clichés. Here's another one I love:

"What does the expression 'The grass is always greener in the other fellow's yard' mean to you?"

"That's easy," dismissed the youngster. "He's using better fertilizer than you are."

And here's another uncut gem in my collection of imaginative jewels:

"Who can tell me how color television works?"

"I can," volunteered a young hand-waver. "It's kind of mixed up, but I know that there's a whole bunch of straws that go from this studio with all kinds of paint, and the straws go to the house and squirt color on the screen."

Can you think of a better explanation? That one makes more sense to me than the diagnosis carefully spelled out by my technical director.

A CHILD'S FAITH in the omniscient powers of good fairies is one of his most appealing qualities, and one which every parent must regretfully watch disappear under the constant attrition of the "growing up" processes. The little ones, themselves, fight with rare imagination the inroads on their private worlds. They dream up some fascinating reasons why there really *could be* leprechauns, and elves, and delightful fairies waiting to surprise them with the good things of this life. And who is to say they are not right, and we wrong to argue the point?

"How'd you lose all those front teeth?" I asked one boy of six.

"They came out in a wad of bubble gum."

"Then what happened?"

"The good fairy brought some money and put it under my pillow."

"Ah," I nodded thoughtfully. "And where does the good fairy get all this money?"

"I think he robs a bank some place!"

The illogical thought of a "good" fairy *robbing* a bank didn't bother him for a moment. Robin Hood lives in many guises and pops up in unexpected places in the thinking of youngsters. Many a strange and devastating anachronism is swallowed whole by a child determined to keep his faith in his good fairy. Take the reply of the young man who was describing a Christmas experience:

"I saw Santa Claus come right over to my bed and hang up a stocking full of presents."

"What did he look like?" I inquired curiously.

"Well, he was wearing pajama tops, and carrying a bottle of beer."

If that was good enough for *him*, it was good enough for *me*. That kind of a Santa Claus is better than *no* Santa Claus.

IT IS ALMOST always obvious to me who the underprivileged children are, and which are the ones who come from homes where there is trouble or unhappiness, regardless of the economic level of that home. They are usually subdued and seem shy and restrained. It is natural for all children to have an exuberance—psychologists say that one of the first things a newborn infant does is to smile. All kids have an innate sense of humor. They want to laugh—at the world, at themselves— but the unfortunate ones are often fearful. They will not venture an answer to a question they don't understand or don't feel sure they know. They will not risk being laughed "at." On the contrary, a child from a secure home, where he is given a firm background of love and understanding, will venture forth bravely on any subject, and if there's a laugh at his answer, he just grins happily in the knowledge that they are *friendly* laughs and he can well afford to join them at his own expense. These well adjusted children have given us some priceless answers:

"What's the difference between a politician and a statesman?" was the question.

◆ "One's running *from* office and one's running *for* it," said a ten year old.

◆ "A politician is always criticizing and a statesman is always criticized," pontificated an eleven year old with surprising wisdom.

◆ "A statesman makes money and the politician spends it," was another calculated guess.

"HOW CAN YOU tell if a person's smart?" was another catchall query.

"Ask him questions, and if he doesn't know the answers he's stupid," dismissed one boy.

"Well, then, let's see how smart you are. Where does the sun go at night?"

"Behind the clouds," he flipped back.

"Then where does the moon come from?" I pressed.

"Well, naturally it gets too hot back of the clouds when the sun goes there, so the moon *has* to come out!" He solved the entire universe and its problems.

Another time I used the expression "Life Begins at Forty" and asked the children if that were true. One little lad said: "Life begins at three for me."

"How is that?"

"Well, three's when school lets out."

HOBBIES ARE FUN to talk about. A child's imagination is vigorously exercised by his hobby because it represents to him an image of his future grown-up life. One youngster told me he was a chemist and had a whole kit g ven him for Christmas.

"Have you made any experiments?" I encouraged him.

"Oh, sure. One time I mixed Ajax, water, saccharine and my Mom's perfume."

"What did you get?"

"I don't know. Just some silly old thing I had to put down the drain." He sighed reflectively at this disaster. Then brightening up, he went on, "But then this summer I ground up some chalk into dust, mixed it with water and got some real crazy Kool-Aid."

A hobby that most young fellows pursue at some time in their lives was frankly admitted by a freckle-faced young guest when he said: "I like to pick fights with my sister." Sensing that I had a "live one" on my hands, I said: "What would your ambition be with this kind of a hobby in your background?"

"Oh, I'd be a rough, tough baseball player," he assured me. "Maybe a left fielder for the Dodgers and an astronomer."

"Wait a minute," I broke in. "What's that 'astronomer' business doing in there with the Dodgers?"

"Well . . . if a baseball hits you in the head you see stars," he grinned at me.

THERE ARE TIMES when the imagination of a young guest puts me in a complete spin. The grave logic of an explanation *sounds* rational as it comes out, but gradually the full impact of its circuitous reasoning comes home with a dull thud. Here's a lulu:

"Anything exciting happen lately around your house?" I began.

"Yes. I hit myself on the back of my head with a hammer."

"That's too bad," I sympathized. "How'd it happen?"

"I wanted to kill a fly."

"Wait a minute," I stopped to reconsider the situation. "How could you *see* him if he was on the *back* of your head where the bump is?"

"He wasn't on the back of my head. He was on the table in front of me."

"But I don't understand," I puzzled. "Then *why* did you hit yourself on the back of the head with the hammer?"

He put his hands on his hips in a gesture of helpless frustration at my stupidity.

"Silly. I wanted to smash him with my *forehead!*"

Anyone who has ever been in trouble has used his imagination to fancy exactly how to get out of it with complete and total impunity. But no one ever topped this girl:

"I'm afraid I'm going to get a bad report card," she admitted.

"What'll happen if you do?" I wondered.

"Oh, I'll get switched good and hard if my folks ever see it. But they won't!"

"Are you sure of that?"

"Yup. I'm going to go down to the harbor and get on a boat and go way out in the ocean and tear it up and throw it to the sharks to eat up." And that finished that!

OCCASIONALLY I ask my young guests what they'd like to tell the world. They have some valuable announcements on their minds almost immediately. Here's proof:

"If anybody's in trouble anywhere in the world, just call my grandpa."

"Who's your grandpa?"

"He's the Sheriff in Utah."

Another optimistic and extremely devious young man had this to say:

"I'm having a birthday party next Saturday. I hope that everyone in the country will come. I live at 200 Walnut Street. The party starts at 2 o'clock. Bring a present!"

And a commercially minded little girl put this plug in for her father:

"All the sick people in the world, if they want to get well can come to my dad. He's a people doctor and he charges $2.00."

SINGLE CHILDREN have always imagined brothers and sisters to be on the way. Many times, parents listening to my broadcasts have been startled to "learn" that a new brother or sister is expected. Some of the young guests have sworn me to secrecy because neither their father nor mother has been told of it yet, and they want it to be a complete surprise when the baby arrives "next week." One strange answer shocked my audience to silence:

"I'd like to have twin sisters. You know, the Siamese kind that are stuck together."

"What in the world do you want with that kind?" I raised my eyebrows into my hair.

"Well, there's three of us in the family already. We only have four chairs at the dinner table. So the new twins could both sit on one chair." That's how simple it was.

Another single child said that he'd be satisfied with a brother.

"Did you ask your Dad about it?" I encouraged him to go on.

"Yep. But he told me to ask my mother."

"What did she say?"

"She just told me to ask my Dad." He seemed despondent.

"What are you going to do next?"

"Well, the only one left to ask is that old bird with the long legs."

SPEAKING OF BIRDS reminds me that a pet is a prime companion for a growing child. I recommend that every little boy and girl be given a chance to care for, train, and live with some sort of animal, fish or bird. Nothing teaches a child so quickly the meaning of responsibility as the assumption of chores related to a living creature and its happiness. But occasionally a good thing can be overdone, as witness this snappy interview in the Peter Lorre idiom:

"Tell us about your pets."

"I had five cats, a dog, and a bird."

"What do you mean *had?* Did something happen to them?"

"Well, first the dog killed almost all the cats." He paused to reflect. "He really wasn't my dog. He lived across the street, and when he came over to see if there was any more cats to kill he got run over."

"What do you have now?" I egged him on.

"We have one bird and one hungry cat."

"Oh-ho," I nodded my head ominously. "Do you know what might happen next?"

"Yes. The cat's going to eat up the bird."

"Then what will you do?"

"Kill the cat." Matter of factly he wrote finis to the whole affair.

Another story of pets that had a tragic note came out of a little sad-eyed girl:

"I used to have a duck but it ran away. Then I had a turtle, but my father stepped on it. Then I had three goldfish, but my sister put water softener in their bowl and they softened to death."

Occasionally a different kind of a tragedy occurs to a pet. To wit:

"I once had a dog, but he got married and moved to Oakland."

OTHER PROBLEMS occur even when the pet stays home safe and sound in the family circle:

"I have a parakeet that likes to play games with me," a six year old volunteered.

"Games?" I puzzled. "What kind of games would a parakeet play?"

"Spelling games. But it's not fair. He can spell all the words I give him. Then he gives me tough words like 'Riverside Drive.' "

If you think *that's* a smart pet, hold it a moment while we focus for a close-up on the optimistic young man who said: "I'd like to have a cocker spaniel because I'm the best animal trainer in the whole world."

"What's the first trick you'd teach him?"

"To stand up on his hind feet on a broom handle."

"You mean the broom handle is lying on the floor?" I couldn't figure this one out.

"No. Up in the air."

"Oh," I nodded understandingly. "Now I get it. You'd hold the broom handle sideways and he'd balance on it?"

"No. He'd stand way up on the end on one paw."

"That's a pretty good one for a starter. What would you teach him next?"

"Oh, I'd think of some *hard* tricks," he assured me.

A more practical pet was dreamed up by a seven year old girl who said she'd like most of all to have a beaver for a chum. When I remarked on such an odd choice, she said:

"No, it isn't. He could sharpen my pencils for me."

Sometimes the hairline decision as to what *is* or what *isn't* a pet evades all but the very young in heart. A snub-nosed youngster put it this way: "I don't have any pets, but I do have a friend." When I asked what kind of a friend, he said:

"An Airedale."

"But isn't that a pet?" I expostulated.

"No, he's a *friend* because he belongs to my next door neighbor."

PEOPLE LISTEN to kids, I think, with a kind of nostalgia. They remember wisps of their own childhood, and recall the blessed times when they could whisk themselves away from the restrictions that society has placed on human beings and do all manner of exhilarating deeds. A six year old recently assured me that someday he was going to drive an armored truck and his Mommy and Daddy would be so proud of him. He went on:

"It's the kind of job where you meet lots of interesting people . . . like bank robbers. And besides that, you make five thousand dollars a week."

"That's a lot of money," I said. "Are you *sure* you get that much?"

"Sometimes more. You just reach back in the truck for what you want."

Come to think of it, this may explain some of those ingenious robberies we've been reading about in the papers lately. This boy may have grown up faster than we know. Another ambitious lad has a breath-taking future all mapped out for him.

"I'm going to be a geometrist," he chattered excitedly. "You know, a fellow who goes out and collects rocks. But I'll have to have another job, too."

"Why another job?"

"Because I'll need the money to support all my wives."

"All *what* wives?"

"Didn't you know? I'm going to move to Siberia where I can have a harem."

ONE OF MY most startling discoveries is that the average American boy is *not* interested in the slightest in becoming President. The great boast of this country: "Any boy can become President," is apparently an empty one. To queries about the possibility of assuming the mantle of leadership, here is what the young fry say:

◆ "If I was President, what would George Washington do?" From a four year old.

◆ "Abraham Lincoln loves every boy and girl. Let's keep *him*," Another four year older.

◆ "I couldn't be President, I don't even know who we're fighting." A sixer.

◆ "You have to work all day, and argue all night. And what about taxes?" Nine year old.

◆ "You have too much responsibility." Now we're up to the eleven year olds.

KIDS WOULD rather be something glamorous and better paid than Presidents. For instance, a seven year old girl wanted to be a sophisticated singer. I asked her, if she were putting on a big show this very night, what she would sing. She thought about it for a moment, and then gravely announced:

'Jesus Loves Me.'

And considering who would be at ringside on a typical Hollywood opening night, I think it's not such a bad suggestion after all. It would be brand new material to most of the customers and quite a novel thought for many.

Of course, as you might suspect, many of the boys dream of being football stars. I posed the calamitous possibility to one youngster of being chased by a 250 pound tackle. What, I supposed, would he do in a terrible situation like that?

"Easy. I'd jump right on his corns." That boy is a future All-American.

Inevitably the job of a fireman is mentioned by a boy in the crowd. The terrible excitement of a fire and the chances for heroism still rate this job at the top of any red-blooded list of future activities. Almost nothing can be said to demean the glories of this job, as I proved one morning when a young man said:

"What fun the firemen have. When the bell rings I jump out of bed and slide down the pole and go to the fire and climb the ladder and get the babies . . ."

"Wait a minute! Wait a minute!" I stopped him in full rescue. "Not so fast there. Let's get back to the fire station. What if there's another fireman ahead of you on the pole?"

"Hah!" he snorted derisively, "every fireman has his own pole!"

THE WHOLE wonder and delight of childhood can be captured by a statement that a darling little girl made to me one morning. It had no startling twist. It had no shock, surprise or "mistake" value. It was simply the shy answer to the question:

"Have you ever been in love?"

"No," she replied, "but I've been in *like*."

You don't have to find any reason for appreciating that. You just do.

Chapter 4

Spinning the Family Circle

"My FAMILY, right or wrong!" This might be the motto you'd find engraved on the subconscious of most growing children. The family circle should encompass the most important areas of a child's world, and represents in the final analysis the kind of thinking, acting, and reacting he will do for the rest of his life. He knows most about this subject and has the strongest opinions about the goings-on under the family roof. This is perhaps the "mother-lode" that an interviewer can mine indefinitely, and the sure-fire, dependable old standby when all else fails.

"What kind of a family have you?" I began the questioning one day.

"Seven children. All girls except one," the six year old sweetie-pie murmured.

"Who's that, your brother?"

"My father."

"Would he like a boy in the family?"

"Yes. But my mother wouldn't."

"Why not?"

"She says that Daddy's enough boy for her!"

And recalling the size of that growing family, I must say I couldn't argue with Mother's viewpoint. Large families are the most fun, I think. My own five youngsters have been a constant source of surprise and delight. And the most surprising thing is that each is so completely different, he might very well have had a different set of parents. Big families, of course, must work out various compromises for adjusting differences and sharing work. I asked one young fellow who had four brothers and three sisters:

"How do you decide who does chores around the house?"

"We have a big council meeting, just like the government."

"Who's President?"

"My mother, of course," he said, surprised that I wouldn't know.

"Who's vice-president?"

"All the rest of us except my dad."

"What's *he*?"

"He's in the living room watching the fights on television."

THE SUBJECT OF housework and household problems finds Dad looking out the window in many families. In fact, it is occasionally the subject for a round-table discussion between several of my young friends. Here are four typical answers:

◆ "My dad doesn't even talk about house-work. He just stays in bed."

◆ "My dad plays golf with the Boss so he'll get a raise."

◆ "My dad won't dust. But he cleans his own teeth."

◆ "My dad won't even come home week-ends if there's any work waiting there."

AND HERE'S A peek into how the youngsters would change their parents if they had a magic wand and could say "Presto! . . . Chango!":

◆ "I'd make them both my size. I don't like big people!"

◆ "I'd make them sweet tempered and rich."

◆ "I'd change my mother and make her skinny in the right places."

◆ "I'd change my dad into a dog and my mom into a cow," was the most startling answer I'd had in a long time. I asked: "Why?"

"Because I like dogs and cows," was the laconic answer. I didn't press *that* subject any further.

HERE'S ONE THAT has echoed and re-echoed through many a home when the first of the month comes around:

"What's your dad's main complaint?"

"My mom's always asking for money."

"What's your mother's main complaint?"

"Dad never gives her any."

And this same off-hand way of summing up a complete family problem is mastered by a seven year old who admitted: "My mother talks most at our house."

"What does your dad do when he can't get a word in edgewise?"

"He gets up and goes to bed."

TRUE CONFESSION Magazine never received such open-faced admissions of guilt as the kids pour out each day about family transgressions. Occasionally I ask: "What were you ever punished for?"

"Taking money from my mother's purse without permission," unhesitatingly he confessed.

"How much did you take?"

"A nickel."

"What did you want it for?"

"A popsicle."

"And what did you get?"

"A spanking."

It takes a lot of patience to bring up a youngster. When I asked one young fellow who had the most patience at his house, he replied: "I would rather not say. If I mention my mother, my dad'll hit me, and if I say my dad, my mother'll hit me."

Child psychology is readily apparent from some of the answers I get. Some parents learn how to use it early and the results are amazing.

"How do you get your parents to say 'yes' when you especially want to do something?"

"I have two magic words," the little girl confided.

"Two magic words! That sounds mysterious," I said. "What are they?"

"Please, and thanks," she smiled up at me.

DRIVING IS A multi-faceted subject because every child is impatiently awaiting his chance to get back of the wheel of the family bus. And like everything else, they are apt to be just as good or bad in their habits as their parents. Do you wonder what sort of traffic conditions will be produced by the child who answered this question:

"Who's the best driver in your family?"

"It's kind of hard to say. My mother always backs part way through the garage. My dad smashed into the end of a parked car yesterday. Last week my mother went up on the curb and knocked an old man down. And they both get hundreds of tickets."

Sounds just like the family that's always driving just ahead of me on the freeway.

When I asked one young man if his daddy talked much while driving, he said, "Yes, he sure does. Are we on the air now?"

"Of course. Why do you ask?"

"Then I'd better not say what Daddy says about the other drivers."

A lisping four year old sprayed me with the following information about his family:

"My fadder works shomeplashe, my mudder works at the house, and my brudder is a shargent over shome sholdiers!"

And another four year old gravely assured me: "Daddy got married because he don't want to do all his own washing and sewing and cooking and dusting or any other work."

A RED HOT topic is the romantic subject of Mother's and Dad's engagement or marriage. From half-remembered, half-overheard, and three-quarters "made-up" facts, the kids concoct some fabulous stories. But they've "shook-up" a lot of staid families, and rattled many an ancestral skeleton. One little tyke murmured the elemental facts:

"How did my daddy and mommy meet? How should I know. I wasn't even borned yet."

A little girl began her story: "My dad had a roommate and my mother had a roommate and they went around together, so they finally arranged a blind date for my mother and dad."

"Was it love at first sight?"

"In a way."

"What way?"

"My dad loved my mother's new car."

Automobiles play quite a part in marriage apparently, because the youngsters tell me of a number of "hit and run" romances. To wit:

"My mother was wheeling her two babies down the street and this man kept driving around the block whistling and flirting. He finally found a parking place, and they got married in March and had me in April."

"My dad was always hanging around where my mother lived because her grandma liked him and wanted my mother to marry him. But she never liked him very much, and probably would never have married him except that he finally got a new hot rod."

How many parents have yelped with pained surprise when they heard family jokes repeated as the gospel truth by the youngsters who tell me everything? I would have enjoyed peeking out through the TV tube into the faces of the Mother and Dad who were immortalized by this answer:

"My dad worked at a vegetable market, and my mother used to come in and pinch

the vegetables. Every time she'd pinch a vegetable, my dad would pinch her until they
couldn't stand it any longer and got married."

Here is an odd-size lot that must have got-
ten a lot of mileage before friends and family mercifully desisted:

"My mother fell over another man into my
father's lap at a party. Somehow they got acquainted, and later they decided to have
some babies so they got married."

AND HERE'S A double handful of assorted
reports on how Dad met Mom and Mom got
Dad:

My daddy and mommy met on a cloud
over Los Angeles.
Then what happened?

I was born on another cloud.
How did you all get down here?
I came down with a raindrop and they
had a double parachute.

◆ ◆ ◆

My folks met in a night club.
What was your father doing?
He was a bartender.
And your mother?
She was attending a PTA meeting.

◆   ◆   ◆

My folks were cousins in Massachusetts, but when they came out to California they had to get married. There's some sort of law out here.

◆   ◆   ◆

How am I supposed to know? I was just a little baby when they were married.

◆   ◆   ◆

Well, this strange man sat down on the bus next to a strange woman, and he said: "Will you marry me?" and she said "yes," and they went home and had me.

One little lad remarked that they had a brand new Daddy around their house. When I asked if he knew how his mother had met him, he told us a real whizzer:

"It all happened one morning when the doorbell rang while Mommy was taking her bath." He stopped to gulp. And at this point I could have inserted a ten minute commercial for any client under the sun and we wouldn't have lost a viewer.

"My little sister went to the door," he finally continued, "and there was a strange man standing there. He said he'd like to see my mother. So sister *let* him!"

No further footnotes were needed to write finis to this bathtub romance.

THE SUBJECT OF remarriage is not a touchy one with the children. They come right out and wish for a new Daddy or Mother with no "ifs," "ands" or "buts." I once asked a little girl: "What kind of a man would you like to have your mother marry?" She said: "I'm not sure, but I think a millionaire."

Another frank guest said: "My mother's busy looking everywhere for a man."

"Where is the best chance to find one?"

"So far, it's best around Santa Monica, she says. But the trouble with most of them is that they yell, or drink or something."

"That's too bad," I consoled him.

"Oh, she doesn't give up easy. She had one a few weeks ago that was just about perfect except for two little things."

"What were those?"

"He didn't like her. And he was already married."

EQUALLY FANTASTIC to the stories of romance, are the guesses about what Mother and Dad do to occupy their time. Here again, the fertile minds of the children play with fragments of truth, putting them together in strange, new patterns that must have made mincemeat out of the nerves of their listening parents. How would you like to have been this boy's mother:

"On Monday my mom cleans the whole house from top to bottom."
"What does she do the rest of the week?"
"Oh, she just sits around, smokes cigarettes and plays canasta."

◆ ◆ ◆

What does your mother do?
  She's a kind of a housewife.
What kind?
  The lazy kind.

◆ ◆ ◆

When does your mother look prettiest?
  When she's going to meet people she doesn't know so good.
And when does she look the worst?
  Around the house in her ragged old nightgown.

◆ ◆ ◆

How old is your mother?
  She says she's thirty, but my dad told me she's really thirty-six.

◆ ◆ ◆

Does your mother work for a living?
  No. She's a private secretary.

Well, that sounds as if she works for a living. Isn't that some kind of a job?

All I know is that she works for a slave driver down in the Fisher Building.

My mother used to sing on television.
Doesn't she do it anymore?
Less and less every day.
Why?
Because every day she gets more and more pregnant.

What does your mother do?
She used to be Laura LaPlante the movie star.
Oh, I remember her, I enthused. What's she doing now?
She's a woman.

What does your mother do?
She's president of the PTA.
That's a very important job. I'll bet she's proud of you, isn't she?
I'll say. And she said to be sure not to say "that damned PTA."

My mother stays home and keeps the dog company.

What kind of a dog is it?

I don't know, but it has one thing the same as my mother.

Are you sure you want to tell us what that is?

Sure . . . it's the same birthday, January 5th!

◆ ◆ ◆

My folks both work. My daddy's a bartender.

And what does your mother do?

Mostly, she goes to the races. Last Sunday, after church, she won $200 on the first race.

Well, that's a nice collection following the sermon, isn't it?

◆ ◆ ◆

My mother's a homemaker, not a house-wife.

Did she tell you to say that?

Yes. 'Cause there's a difference. You know the saying, "a happy homemaker and a nagging housewife."

◆ ◆ ◆

My mother's in ladies underwear in the basement.

That's a strange thing to say. What do you mean?

She works for the May Company.

◆ ◆ ◆

My mother likes to work crossword puzzles. She's real good.

How many does she do a week?

None. She's just real good at starting them. The family always has to finish.

My mother keeps saying, "Boot it out and do it over again."
What does that mean?

Oh, we're remodeling the house and that's what she says to the builders every day.

My mother sculptures with no clothes on.
Doesn't she get cold?

No, silly, the *other* people are the bare ones.

AND FINALLY, here are a few random descriptions of mothers, which constitute the complete, total answer to the question: "How would I know your mother if I met her?"

◆ "My mother has black suede shoes and clean pants."

◆ "My mother has a brown dress, brown shoes and long stockings with knots in them to hold them up above the knee."

◆ "My mother's sort of fat and wears a torn green dress."

◆ "My mother wears a funny Chinese nightgown with a slit up the sides so she has to wear pants under it."

◆ "My mother has dark brown hair, glasses and a lot of safety pins where you can't see them."

IN SPITE OF everything that television and movies can do to make All-American Father look like the All-Time Boob, he's still okay with Junior. In fact, Junior is liable to invent a pedestal for Dad that makes the Old Boy a trifle uncomfortable by its size and shiny elegance. Many times each month my school teacher hands me a note with stories of bravery and derring-do as told to her on the way to the studio by bragging youngsters. One boy's father is a policeman who arrests burglars by the score. Another girl's dad is a fireman or a jet pilot or a deep sea diver who makes each day an adventurous saga. And then, under the cold eye of the TV camera, that same little boy or girl will answer my question about Daddy: "He's a plumber." In fact, the kids make the transition from truth to fiction with such an imperceptible jolt that I'm never sure whether I'm being kidded, or whether he's kidding himself. Quite often it's a bit of both, which makes for fun at the family TV set. Here's one:

"What does your dad do?"

"He's a got a swell job at the Hall of Justice." He looked around a trifle nervously.

"He shoots people who are bad and come to steal money from the government."

"Isn't he ever scared?" I egged him on.

"Never." He stood by this wild tale resolutely.

"How do you know?" I persevered.

"My mother wouldn't let them hurt him. She's got a great big old French butcher knife hidden in the kitchen under the sink."

Another young fellow had a different reason for thinking his dad was a Big Wheel.

"My dad's got an important job out at Douglas," he stated.

"How do you know he's important?"

"Well, he has a pretty secretary that my mother's always yelling at him about."

Then, there's always a boy in the crowd who sees a chance to use one of his dad's jokes when I pop the question. Here's a sample:

"My dad's got a stinking job. He works in a sewerage plant."

OF COURSE, THE complete truth is likely to cause a change in Dad's occupation if the Boss is listening. And I suspect that many a new relationship has been formed following the revelation of "inside" information relayed like a triple play from Dad to Junior to Television. I wonder, for instance, where a film writer is now working whose little boy said: "Daddy wrote the story for the movie *Escape at Night,* but the studio messed the whole thing up and made a lousy picture."

And what about the innocent who spouted: "My Dad's a cop who arrests burglars, robbers and thieves."

When I said, "Doesn't your mother worry about such a risky job?" he answered, "Naw, she thinks it's a great job. He brings home rings, and bracelets and jewelry almost every week."

This might be a clue to the Senate Investigating Committee as to a new method for arriving at the truth about racketeers, smugglers, and dishonest officials!

Less severe, but nonetheless nerve-shaking would be the following revelation:

"My Dad's a cop that rides in a patrol car, except he doesn't like it."

"Why not?"

"Because he'd rather be with all the rest of the guys back at the station, drinking, playing cards, and listening to the radio."

Another complaint in behalf of a policeman father was registered by a young man who said: "The prisoners all call him 'flatfoot.'"

"What does your dad do about it?"

"That's what makes him mad. He can't do anything. They're already in jail."

I LOVE THE bravado of the entire family represented by this father's attitude: The son said, "My Dad's the bravest man alive. A lot of people are going to sue him, but he don't care."

Other attitudes of carefree, irresponsible fathers are italicized by the crisp comments of their offspring who say:

"My dad's a doctor and he sure hates to be bothered by all the calls from sick people, especially at dinnertime and everything gets cold."

"What can he do about it?" I argued. "After all he's a doctor."

"He changes the phone number and doesn't tell them, so they can't find him."

And here's another in the same vein:

"My Dad's a termite man who crawls into attics and under houses and finds those bugs that eat up houses and kills them."

"Have you ever seen a termite?"

"Oh, sure, we have them all over the place where we live."

"Won't they eat up your house?" I was astonished. "Isn't your dad worried?"

"Why should he care; we're renters!"

This next bit of philosophy is something I've often thought about when I've read about some clever criminal beating the rap. It's put so perfectly:

"My father's a good lawyer."

"Just what *is* a good lawyer?"

"He gets bad people out of jail."

And here's one that the family will be reminded of at every party they go to for the next few years. I had asked a young lady how her father could be better.

"I hope he stops putting his cold legs on Mommy's back."

Incidentally, one youngster assured me that a good father is supposed to be "obedient, prompt, courteous, generous, kind, and cooperative." When I asked her where she got all those ideas, she promptly said: "They're right here on my report card."

GOING OVER THE tape recordings of a few dozen of my favorite shows, I screened out a few of the choicest descriptions of "Dear Old Dad" and how he spends his time. Here they are for your amusement:

◆ ◆ ◆

What does your daddy do?
    Washes rags.
Is that a good business?
    Well, we know who has the dirtiest rags in town. But I'm not supposed to tell.

◆ ◆ ◆

    My daddy spreads joy.
To whom?
    To anybody who can pay for it.
I don't understand what kind of a job he has.
    He's a bartender.
I'll bet somebody put you up to this?
    My mother. She's always joking and *drinking beer*.
(And there the joke turned on dear old Mother.)

◆ ◆ ◆

My father's a school teacher.
That's a fine profession. Does he like it?
He only has one thing to complain about.
What's that?
The kids.

◆ ◆ ◆

My dad's a professor of English at a college.
What does he think of the students?
Well, he tells me the best student in his class is a beautiful blonde girl with blue eyes and a tight sweater.

◆ ◆ ◆

My father's a nurseryman and raises flowers.
What sort?

Algerians.
Algerians? I repeated foggily.
Yes, red ones, white ones and pink ones.
Don't you mean geraniums? I corrected her.
Yes, Algerians.

◆ ◆ ◆

My dad's a cop and a bartender. He's sure busy.

How can he do both of those jobs?

Well, first he gets the people happy and then arrests them.

My dad's a fireman and he sure likes his job.

What's he like best about it?

All the big fires happen on his day off.

My father's the bravest man in the world.

How do you know?

He cut his finger on a glass one time and didn't even cry.

What was he doing?

He was down in the basement bottling beer.

My dad comes home mad every day.

What makes him so sore?

He's a waiter in Hollywood for all the movie stars.

What's so bad about all that?

They're all so rich and they leave such small tips.

My father's a physigist. It's something with electrons.

How do they work? Do you know?

Well, it's like two coke bottles with stuff inside them so that when it comes out and goes across between them, all of a sudden there's nothing.

Oh. That must be interesting work. And what about your mother?

She's the Dean of Women at the college.

Is that a difficult job?

She just goes to faculty luncheons.

With all of this brain power in your family tree, what profession will you follow?

A plumber.

My daddy brings home ice cream all the time. He works in an ice cream factory.

What's the best flavor?

My mother likes chocolate. Mine is vanilla. My brother's is strawberry, and my sister's is pistachio.

How about your dad?

He hates ice cream.

My father's a dentist.

Then I suppose you'll be a dentist, too?

Naw. It's too gooey a job. The people yell too much. I'm going to be a doctor.

What if I came to you with a broken arm, what would you do?

Put it in a cast.

What if I had a stomachache?

I'd give you a pill.
And what if I had a hole in my head?
I'd put a cork in it!

◆ ◆ ◆

So your dad's a fireman. Does he tell you any exciting stories about big fires?
The most excitement is right at the fire station.
What happened there?
A fireman heard the bell, jumped out of bed, pulled on his pants, slid down the pole upside down and knocked himself out when he hit the bottom.

◆ ◆ ◆

My mother thinks my dad has a wonderful job. He's a fireman.
What's so good about that?
She thinks it's wonderful. He works for 24 hours and then he's off for 24 hours. That means she can get him out of the house and get her housework done every other day.

◆ ◆ ◆

My dad's a policeman and the best shot on the force.
Did he get a medal?
No, he got a man.

◆ ◆ ◆

My father's an electronics scientist.

Would you care to explain further?

Well, I have to be careful of my pronunciation. He's a thinker.

My dad's as busy as a beaver.

That's an interesting figure of speech. Do you know what that means?

Well, you know how beavers are always cutting down trees with their teeth . . .

Is that what your dad does? I broke in abruptly.

Oh, he's not really a beaver. Besides, he has false teeth.

My dad's a lawyer.

Does he put people in jail?

No, he's on the innocent side.

I suppose you want to be a lawyer?

No, a cop, so I can put my daddy in jail.

Why would you do a thing like that?

He spanked me last night.

So your dad's a minister. So was mine. Is he a good minister?

He must be a pretty smooth talker.

Why?

Because on Sundays almost everybody goes to sleep but me and mother.

Doesn't that make your dad mad?

Not nearly as mad as the collections. He gets two offerings and the trouble is he's got a cheap congregation and most of them put in pennies.

Having grown up as the son of an evangelist who depended for the family livelihood on the collections, I can appreciate that answer more than most. In fact, my first appearance in public was for the purpose of helping swell the Sunday offering. Dressed in neat, patched clothes, I would solemnly parade up and down the church aisles with the plate, while my father beamed down from the pulpit and encouraged everyone to "dig deep, brothers and sisters, for the good work." Even at this late date, I can still look appraisingly out over an audience and guess within a few dollars the kind of collection we'd get.

◆　◆　◆

How are you going to be a better boy during the coming year?

Obey everybody in my family except my Aunt Freda.

Why not her?

Cause she just causes trouble and starts fights.

How old is she?

Eight.

◆　◆　◆

What's your name?

Rudigore Sitka.

With that kind of name, what kind of blood do you have in you?

Red.

I mean where did your mother and father come from?

Well, on my mother and father's side there's a little of Chicken-slovakian, some Yugoslavian, some French, a small hunk of Jewish and English and Scotch and I think there's one drop of Cherokee Indian.

◆ ◆ ◆

Did you take a bath last night?

Nope.

Why not?

Because I'm saving the soap for my dad. He's the dirty one in the family.

◆ ◆ ◆

What do you do when you come home from school?

Go to bed.

And what does your dad do?

Same thing.

And your mother?

She sleeps all the time.

◆ ◆ ◆

Anybody tell you anything to do today?

Some of my mother's best friends called me and told me to tell you that all my mother does all day long is to yak on the phone and play bridge.

Did you say your mother's best friends?
  Well, they *were*.

◆ ◆ ◆

What does your mom do?
  She's a Sunday School teacher.
What does she do for fun?
  She plays poker and drinks beer.

◆ ◆ ◆

Where'd you get that blond hair?
  Well, it's like my mother's used to be.
What happened?
  She dyed it brown and it came out purple.

◆ ◆ ◆

Why did you get to come today?
  Because my mother tells me that I'm intelligent and have a wonderful personality.

◆ ◆ ◆

Did you get any instructions from home today?
  Yes.
What were they?
  Not to eat sloppy and burp.

◆ ◆ ◆

Did your mother tell you anything not to say today?
  Yes; that I shouldn't tell about my dad gambling at Las Vegas because his boss might be listening in.
Then maybe we'd better get off the subject and talk

*about something else. Where do you want to go for
your vacation this year?*

Las Vegas.

*Let's try something else. What do you want to be
when you grow up?*

I want to be a child star now, retire when
I'm 30, and when I'm 50 go to an old lady's
home in Las Vegas.

◆ ◆ ◆

*Your last name's Panetroveo . . . what kind of a
name is that?*

That's a regular American name.

How do you know?

I was born in the county hospital.

◆ ◆ ◆

What's your name?

Nancy Mottler.

What kind of name is that?

True American; a little bit of everything.

◆ ◆ ◆

How many teeth have you lost?

Three, so far.

When does it bother you?
   When I try to eat an apple.
How do you do it?
   My dad starts it for me.

◆   ◆   ◆

What's your favorite expression?
   "Oh, you lop-eared knucklehead."
Who's that?
   Me.
Who calls you that?
   My dad.

◆   ◆   ◆

Where were you born?
   Los Angeles.
How long ago?
   I don't know; nobody'll tell me.

◆   ◆   ◆

What does it mean when you say "He's a dumb bunny?"
   That's a man who never gives his wife any money to spend.

◆   ◆   ◆

What do you want to be?
   Oh, a hundred things.
What mainly?
   A housewife.
What does your mother say to that?
   She says "don't be a housewife because no

matter what else you are you won't have as much trouble."

I want to be a nurse and have all ladies for patients.
Why not men?
Because they complain too much.
How do you know?
Because Daddy complains all the time about Mommy taking his money.

Where does your father work?
At the Sufferin Pacific.
Don't you mean Southern Pacific?
No, I mean Sufferin Pacific 'cause that's what my dad does there.

Your first name is Sherrin . . . how did you get that spelling?
When my mother named me she wasn't in her right mind.
How do you mean?
She was still under ether.

Mother made my dress.
How did you help?
I didn't wiggle.

With that name, what are you?

Half Swedish, half Texan, half Scotch and half American.

What do you think you'll be when you grow up?

According to my mother, I'll be a lawyer, probably.

What makes you think so?

Well, my mother says I talk so much all the time I might as well be a lawyer and get paid for it.

What will you be when you grow up?

A general in the Army.

What does your dad do?

He's a master sergeant.

What's the difference between that and a general?

A general gets more money, more food and more sleep.

What do you want to be?

A traffic cop.

Ever see one up close?

I'll say! The other day Dad got a ticket for going through a stop signal and when the cop came up to the car I helped him. I told him that Dad hadn't been looking.

Chapter 5

Bugging the Family

A PRIVATE EYE once told me that he had been bugging people's homes for years and that he'd never yet found a family that could afford to have its privacy exposed to the public view. Imagine how *you'd* feel if you learned that a wiretap had been hidden in your house for the last few years and that your most intimate conversations were to be broadcast over a national network!

There *is* such a hidden mike in millions of homes throughout this land of ours. It's called a child. And it picks up everything it hears—and repeats it when the right questions are asked.

My job for twenty-five years was to ask the right questions on my CBS *House Party* show. And I suppose as a result of some of the candid answers, many families moved away and relocated under another name!

My all-time favorite involved the boy who answered my question about what his parents did for fun by saying, "Search me; they always lock the bedroom door."

Another youngster said, "The most fun at my house is in the morning when I pull down my dad's pants while he's shaving."

A six year old girl solemnly assured me that she never has any fun because she has no sisters to play with. I wondered if she had talked to her mother about it, and she said "Yes, and Mommy says we'll get one the minute Daddy gets rested up!"

PERHAPS the most remembered bombshell was dropped during World War II when I was talking to a young lad whose father was overseas in military service. Hoping to console him for his Dad's absence I said, "I know you're lonesome for your Daddy, but don't worry, he'll be back home soon, I'm sure, safe and sound." The six year old corrected me promptly and effectively: "Oh, no, I think it's great. I get to sleep with Mommy every night except Wednesdays when Uncle Bob comes over!"

That story has been repeated to me by more people over the years than any other, and it's amazing how much the stories vary, with every kind of imagined frills added! I thought it was startling enough in its direct, right-on-the-button approach. Incidentally, though, I did hear a variation of this story that I'd like to pass along. It seems that Daddy was a traveling businessman whose frequent trips kept him away from home for several nights at a time. On these occasions, Mother kept her mischievous brood of four kids in line by promising that the one who caused no trouble each day during Daddy's absence would be rewarded by being allowed to sleep with Mother in the big bed that night. On this particular two-day trip, nobody had behaved well, and when the family went to the airport to pick up the returning husband, the eight year old rushed ahead of the group yelling to the approaching father at the top of his excited voice, "Daddy, Daddy, no one slept with Mother while you were gone!"

OF COURSE, some of my young visitors suspected there were family secrets that shouldn't be revealed, but they were willing to make a guess as to the nature of the hush-hush subject.

"Any special secrets in your house?" I asked one five year old doll. "Well," she speculated, "Mommy won't tell me, but I think I'm going to get a baby brother." "What makes you think that?" I pursued. "Daddy just keeps getting fatter and fatter every day!"

Even more startling was the speculative shot fired by a little boy who was asked what his Daddy did and replied "I don't have a Daddy. He went away when I was just a baby." "Oh," I sympathized, "then you are the only child in your family?" "No," he blithely replied, "I have two baby brothers. We don't have a Daddy. I guess Mamma just does the best she can."

Here, now, are a few more of my favorite examples of what happens when a small innocent ventures out too far on a limb of the family tree.

Richard, what's your dad's biggest problem?
   Tequila.
Oh, then, your father drinks?
   No, Tequila's our dog.

◆   ◆   ◆

What's your dad?
   A mechanic.
What does your mother do?
   Nothing special.
How many brothers and sisters do you have?
   Ten brothers and seven sisters.
And your mother does "nothing special?"
   No, she just lays around the house.
I don't blame her!

◆   ◆   ◆

What's your dad do?
   He's a conductor on a train.
How does he like it?
   Fine, except once in a while he gets mad.
When is that?
   When the train leaves without him.

◆   ◆   ◆

What does your dad do?
   He's a dry cleaner.

Fine. Now can you tell me who is the President of the U.S.?

Sure. Abraham Lincoln.

Where does he live?

I don't know; we never pick up any of his clothes.

◆ ◆ ◆

Is your dad handy around the house?

He sure is.

What did he ever fix?

My mother's back.

◆ ◆ ◆

Tell us about your Mother and Dad.

Dad's a minister and Mom's just a housewife.

What does your dad do for fun?

He rings the church bell on Sunday.

And what does your Mother do for fun?

I don't know; she's expecting.

EVERY FAMILY seems to have its private jokes. Those funny and sometimes racy explanations of how the parents met, or fell in love. The catch is that their trusting offspring hear those gags around the house and take them for gospel truth. Then, when the kid blurts it out on my show, the gag is on dear old Mom and Dad!

Bobby, how did your folks meet and get married?

Ha, ha. That's funny. They aren't even married!

◆ ◆ ◆

Jimmy, how did your folks meet?

They were both poor, but my Mom owned a bathtub and she let my Dad share it with her.

◆ ◆ ◆

Charlotte, did your parents have a romantic meeting and fall in love?

Boy, I'll say so. Dad drove a milk truck and when he came along one morning there was Mom, waiting, sitting on an empty milk bottle!

◆ ◆ ◆

Ronnie – did you ever hear how your folks fell in love?

It was kind of exciting. They were both Marines in the war. Mom was in the top bunk and Dad was in the bottom bunk and they kept running into each other when they got up in the morning.

◆ ◆ ◆

Freddy, who do you look like in the family?

Nobody. Daddy says I look like the milkman. Mama says I look like the plumber. But I think I look most like the preacher!

◆ ◆ ◆

Robby, do you want to be like your Daddy when you grow up?

You betcha. He's a bachelor and I guess that's lots of fun.

(His mother looked me up after the show to red-facedly explain that Daddy just got his Bachelor's degree at UCLA.)

PARENTS usually enjoy a joke on themselves as much as the audience does. Naturally Dad laughs the loudest when Mother is the butt of the joke, and vice versa. But sometimes a child launches a shaft with such deadly accuracy that it brings a yelp from the parent that can literally be heard from coast to coast. Like this:

"Would you describe your mother?"

"Well, she used to have blonde hair but she's dyed it red so often it's falling out." At this point a muffled shriek was heard from a red-haired lady in the audience. "What was that?" I asked. "I guess it was my Mom. She always yells when I tell family secrets."

One of the surest ways to get a glimpse of a child's family life is to ask him who's boss around the house. So, let's see how dear old Dad is doing:

Who's the boss in your family?

My dad.

Why do you think so?

Because if I want to go somewhere and I ask my Dad and he says yes, then I can go if my Mom lets me.

◆ ◆ ◆

Why do you think your dad is boss, Sharon?
Well, I'm not real sure, but I think it's because he sits at the head of the table.

◆ ◆ ◆

Movie star Lloyd Bridges is a fearless hero to millions of his fans on the screen but when I asked his daughter Sandy "who's the real boss in your family?" she said, "Daddy's the boss in the movies. Mom's the boss at home."

◆ ◆ ◆

Another girl told me her Dad was an officer in the Marine Corps so I asked, "What's his rank?"
"What's that mean?"
"How important is he?"
"Search me. Around our house, Mom's boss!"

◆ ◆ ◆

Who's boss in your family?
Dad. He won't even wear the shorts my Mom buys for him because they're too tight.
Then what happens?
She gives them to my uncle. He doesn't like 'em either.

Is there an end to this story?
  Yep, my aunt wears 'em.

◆ ◆ ◆

Where does your daddy work, Sammy?
  In a marriage clinic.
Does anything ever upset a marriage counselor?
  Yeah. Mom's yelling and screaming.
Who's she screaming at?
  Dad.

HAVE YOU ever wondered how the wizards of the financial world would do at home with their own family budgets? Listen:
  "What's your Dad, Steve?
  "A banker."
  "And how would you describe your family?"
  "Just average."
  "What do you mean, 'average'?"
  "We owe everybody."

◆ ◆ ◆

Ten year old Jenny gave us a start when she said:
  My Dad's in the burglary business.
You mean he robs people?
  No, he owns the U.S. Burglar Alarm Company.
How's business?
  Wonderful. There are robberies going on everywhere.

◆ ◆ ◆

"What's your Dad do, Lois?"

"He tells me he's a life saver, but I don't believe him."

"Why not?"

"Because Mama told me he just works in a dry cleaning plant taking lipstick marks out of men's collars."

◆　◆　◆

"How about your Dad?"

"He's a cop."

"What's his biggest problem?"

"He says it's crazy women drivers."

"Who's the best driver in your family?"

"My Mom."

◆　◆　◆

"Karen, what's your family like?"

"My Dad's fat, my grandmother's fat, my Mom's skinny. I guess my dog has the best shape of anybody."

◆　◆　◆

"Do you look like your Mother, young lady?"

"No, sir—no way."

"What do you mean 'no way?'"

"I don't have false eyelashes, false teeth, or false hair. And I don't wear any falsies, either!"

◆　◆　◆

SEVEN year old Karen told me all about her big family and the rules they've worked out for the morning routine. She said:

"First my Mother gets up and goes to the bathroom, and when she gets out she wakes my sister and *she* goes to the bathroom, then she wakes another sister and *she* goes to the bathroom, then my sister wakes my brother and he goes to the. . . ."

"That's enough!" I interrupted. "We get the idea."

◆ ◆ ◆

Another little girl with three brothers and four sisters revealed what good manners are in a family as large as hers:

"Don't run around eating anything gooey, don't yell before the sun comes up, and don't leave the toilet seat up."

◆ ◆ ◆

Eight year old Bobby obviously comes from a thrifty—and shifty—kind of family. I asked him:

"What's the most important rule in your family?"

"If you make a phone call anywhere, always reverse the charges."

WHATEVER ELSE kids are, they're not sophisticated about humor. They like to *see* the joke happen. I guess that's why clowns are the favorite part of any circus to a kid. Anyway, I've had some of my best laughs asking the kids to tell me the funniest sights they've ever seen around the house:

◆ "My Dad tried to open a bottle of beer, and the top flew up and hit him in one eye and the beer squirted up in his other eye. Boy, he was a mess!"

◆ "My Mom tried on all her underpants and they were too small so she tried on Daddy's and they didn't fit either."

◆ "My Mother looked like a wriggly old snake getting into her new girdle. And when she finished, she looked real good except for the parts that hung over."

◆ "My Mother wearing my dad's pajamas so he has to go to bed without them."

◆ "When my little brother was playing with the dog and the dog bit him, so he bit the dog back and ran out of the house yelping." "Your brother?" "No, the dog."

◆   ◆   ◆

I GUESS one of my favorite all-time questions is: "How did your Mother and Dad meet and fall in love?" The variety and originality of the stories that came from the lips of the kids were staggering:

◆ "My Mom worked in a real estate office and Dad was going to buy a bum house filled with termites. She tipped him off and he was so grateful he married her."

◆ "My Dad was walking down this street and he fainted, and my Mother came along and dragged him into a drugstore. So Dad said the only way he could pay her back was to drag her to the altar."

◆ "My Dad was in the Navy and Mom was always there when the ship came in, to help with the anchor or something."

◆ "My Dad married my Mom when her Daddy told him there was a law and he ought to."

◆ "I don't know *how* they met . . . but I'm glad they did!"

◆ "My Dad was a boss, and my Mom worked for him. He kept chasing her around the desk until he finally caught her. And here I am."

◆ "My Daddy was a lifeguard at this big swimming pool, where my Mom lost her swimming suit. I don't know what happened then, but they got married."

Chapter 6

Bombshells Away!

UNEMBARRASSED directness—those two words represent the double distilled essence of a child's charm. Take, for example, the unblinking, wide-eyed honesty of a five year old discussing the part of the Holy Bible he most enjoys:

"I like the part where Moses breaks all the Ten Commandments!"

When you know that a kiddie's remarks are uttered in complete innocence, then any embarrassing mistakes, penetrating truths, or horrifying revelations must not only be forgiven by the rest of us but enjoyed as a rare treat.

Who can complain about the little girl's earnest ambition:

"I want to be a secretary when I grow up. Unless I have a baby. Then, I'd like to be married!"

Or who can criticize the young fellow who was recalling the most exciting part of his summer camping trip:

"We didn't know where we were so we just unrolled our sleeping bags and Daddy told us to climb right in with our clothes on and go to sleep. What we didn't know was that we were camping right next to a railroad track that went through this farm. Then in the middle of the night, a big train went right by our beds. Gosh, was it exciting! I went to the bathroom right there in my sleeping bag!"

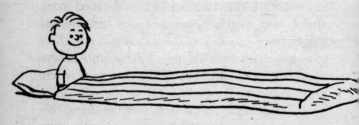

Children are most apt to be most direct with other children. No namby-pamby talk is heard when forthright opinions are indicated. My own seven year old Robert was no exception to the rule, as overheard in the opening conversation with a brand new neighbor through our connecting fence.

"I think I'll climb over and play with your wagon," announced little Sammy as the opening gambit.

"Oh, yeah," replied Robert quietly. "Just come over and you'll see what happens."

"Oh, yeah!" sneered Sammy. "So what'll happen?"

"I'll cut you up in little round pieces, stuff you down our toilet. And then," in a triumphant crescendo, "I'll flush you away!"

My outraged yelp from the porch shattered this prelude to open warfare, and I followed it with a stern lecture to my young son.

"How many times have I told you?" I remonstrated. "Never, never, never, stuff anything down that toilet! Plumbers cost money!"

BEFORE YOU SNICKER at the red-faced parents whose small fry have spilled the beans, consider for a moment if you could stand to have an inquisitive six year old spend a few months at *your* house and then report what he had seen and heard to a nationwide television audience. Many a parent realizes too late how really big those little rascal's ears can be! And how much of what they see and hear comes out strangely garbled.

I'll never forget the boy who told me that his mother had cautioned him not to say anything silly or preposterous. When I inquired about what kind of silly things he could possibly say, he replied: "Well, for one thing, she told me to be sure not to tell you that she's pregnant."

"What's so silly about that?" I commented kindly.

"Because she *ain't!*" He put the period on that interview!

Children tell the truth in the fewest possible words. There is no gentle preamble. There is no introductory "warm up." They reveal situations entire. For example, this one — a little girl:

"Any brothers and sisters?"

"No."

"Would you like some?"

"Sure, I'm lonesome."

"What does your mother say when you ask for one?"

"She just groans."

And there was the little boy whose hair was, to put it mildly, very odd.

"Who gave you that trick haircut?"

"My grandpa."

"Is he a pretty good barber?"

"He's not a barber. He's a carpenter."

SOMETIMES THE conversation takes a serious turn. Ponder this short exchange with a little boy from an underprivileged home:

"Where do you sleep when company comes, if you have only one bedroom?"

"Under the bed with all the dirt and dust."

Perhaps my handling of children from poor homes is understandable because I lived in poverty when I was a youngster. My father was not a practical man. He made a little money at a variety of occupations; he never kept it. Finally he even gave up trying to make it. He had always been religious; he became an itinerant evangelist and preached on street corners. My mother and I lived where we could, on such money as my father was able to collect from his "offerings" and send to us. Once we occupied one room in an old people's home. Most of the rooms we had were skimpy and bare. Christmas and Thanksgiving would have been bleak if churches hadn't donated our dinners. I was the last one of the neighborhood gang to have a bike; the first one to have a paper route. So the sympathy and friendship I feel for any underprivileged child is very real because of these things. Nevertheless, the unfortunate kids also have childhood's gift for telling the truth most surprisingly. I remember particularly a shabbily dressed little boy whom I asked: "What makes a happy home?"

His reply was quick: "A steady pay check."

The answer, however wry it is in context, still has humor. Adults would have fumbled and stumbled around with complicated and involved answers. The little boy went straight to fundamentals. Another matter-of-fact child was the little girl who told me her parents had saved up especially so she could look nice for the program. She elaborated:

"I have on a new dress, new shoes, socks and

a slip. The only thing really *old* I have on is my pants and nobody's going to see them anyway!"

THE "ETERNAL war of the siblings" is a pat phrase of child psychologists, and as any parent will admit, the conflict between brothers and sisters is *indeed* an everlasting one. No only child will ever understand how many battles he has missed under the family roof by not having to share food, toys, clothes and "Lebensraum" with a hotly competitive brother. And the kids are the first to admit it. There's no hedging when the subject comes up.

"Any brothers or sisters?"

"One sister."

"What kind of a sister is she?"

"A big fat slob!"

Sometimes I wince when I conjure up the picture around the family TV set when this kind of answer is blurted out. "Sister" must either kick the tube out, or run for the garage to select the proper size baseball bat for "brother's" homecoming. Even the tiny humanitarians among my guests deviate from their noble purpose in life when

brothers or sisters are mentioned. A dedicated little "nurse" stated:

"I want to help all the sick people in the world. I'll give shots to little boys and girls to keep them well. If they're good I'll give them shots in the arm. If they're bad like all my brothers and sisters, they'll get the shots in the bottom!"

Another philanthropist was ruminating about what he'd do with a million dollars:

"First, I'd get a swimming pool. Then a yellow Cadillac. I'd buy a big house. I'd give a little money to some poor people if I could find them. And I'd put my big brother on a leaky old ship in the middle of the Atlantic Ocean."

Older brothers and sisters elicit a different type of frankness that must startle friends, relatives, and possibly sweethearts. Listen to this bold recital:

"I have a big brother in the Army 'way up in Alaska."

"That must be exciting," I replied. "Does he write about all the news up there?"

"Naw! All I know is he has an Eskimo girl friend."

THE MODERN FAMILY is apparently discussing all manner of things before the small fry. Scientific and medical words and phrases pop up unconcernedly in casual conversation over TV which must cause mouths to fly open from San Diego to Bangor, Maine. Parents who have reeled back from the TV screen, aghast at their child's revelations, later collect the remnants of their sanity and confess that they, themselves, are to blame for speaking so frankly. What a child hears he repeats. Especially when Mother and Dad sanction it by their own usage. Fasten your seat belts for this one:

"What do you want to talk about Suzanne?"

"Oh, anything. Let's talk about my operations."

"Your operations?" I echoed. "Let's see . . . you're six. How many operations have you had?"

"Quite a few."

In my innocence I went on: "For instance?"

"Well, there was adenoids, tonsils, my teeth filled, my eyes tested and I got circumcised!"

She smiled up sweetly at me, waiting for the next question, while the audience fell into the aisles partly from this verbal bombshell exploding so unexpectedly, and partly from the dazed glassy-eyed look of a pole-axed steer that spread over my face.

Finally, gathering some inner strength, I murmured politely: "Yes, you *have* lived dangerously!" . . . And moved on to safer territory elsewhere.

Similarly, most children over five regard childbirth with very little mystery or concern. One little fellow assured me he had no brothers or sisters, and didn't expect any. When I asked him how he could be so sure, he shrugged nonchalantly, and said:

"Because my mother's not pregnant."

THE OWNERSHIP of a pet also gives the modern child a clear, straight look at life in the raw. Like farm children who grow up surrounded by the everyday miracle of birth and death and procreation, the city boy or girl takes for granted the fundamental activities and problems of living creatures. I personally approve of this attitude wholeheartedly, although at times it rattles me for a moment on the air.

"How could you be a better boy?" I asked one six year old fellow.

"If I brushed my teeth every morning instead of just at night."

"And why don't you brush your teeth in the morning?"

"Because the first thing I have to do when I get up is to clean up after my dog, and after that I just don't feel like brushing my teeth."

Another prime example of directness is found in this simple, one-line dialogue:

"Any pets?"

"Eleven cats."

"Why so many?"

"We just had a mother and a daddy cat and we couldn't stop them in time."

And imagine this clinical talk from a *five* year old:

"I used to have a dog, but he's gone."

"What happened to him?"

"One night I let him out to defecate and he ran away."

Even the elemental laws of supply and demand are underscored in a frank and open way by the child who is talking about his pet. One young man told me that he had something better than a brother or a sister. He had a mama dog.

"How many puppies does she have?"

"That was the trouble." He wrinkled up his forehead in disgust.

"What was the trouble?"

"She had nine puppies and only eight nipples!"

NAMES OF animals bring out some rather direct reasoning. Especially when the youngster is allowed to help in the selection. One young fellow told me his dog was named "Puddles." Sensing the basis for this choice I went on to something else, but this didn't satisfy his pride of ownership. Butting in to my next question, he went on:

"We thought 'Puddles' was a good name because that's what he makes all over the whole house."

Names often have very little relation to the fundamental differences in animals. Try to follow this line of reasoning and see if you could improve on it:

"Any pets?"

"A collie dog named George."

"Is he a good dog?"

"George is a 'she'."

"Oh," I paused a moment to digest this contradictory bit of news. "Well, then, what does *she* do, mostly?"

"She plays with our cat, Mopsy."

"Is she a good cat?"

"Mopsy is a *he*."

"Now wait a minute," I cautioned. "Aren't you a little confused?"

"Sometimes. But *they* never are!"

And neither was this little boy confused who paid his first visit to a farm on a summer vacation. When I asked him what he saw there of interest, he replied:

"A whole big bunch of cows and just one bull."

"That's nice."

"Yes . . . my uncle says that's all they need."

Speaking of farms reminds me of the shock a doting uncle must have received one day a few years ago when a young guest admitted that he'd like to grow up to be a farmer.

"What kind of a farmer?"

"A gentleman farmer," he volunteered.

"Are you sure you know what a gentleman farmer *is*?" I pressed. "What do they *do*?"

"Nothing!" he smiled in anticipation. "That's what I like about it."

"How do you know?"

"My favorite uncle Eddie is one, Daddy says."

I WONDER WHAT would happen in the great game of politics if the Republican and Democratic campaigners were to be as direct and frank about their real feelings as a young guest of mine recently. This is exactly what he said:

"We're electing a new student body president at school."

"What's your job? Are you helping out?"

"I'm campaign manager for Larry."

"Larry who?"

"I don't know his last name. I'm just his campaign manager."

"I'd like to hear what you have to say about this Larry What's-his-name. How did your campaign speech go?"

"I'm not one of those fellows that makes long speeches. I just want to tell you that Larry is the best man for the job and you should vote for him. That's all."

"That's one of the best political speeches I ever heard," I applauded him. "Who's Larry's opponent in the big race?"

"Yokl."

"Who are you voting for?"

"Yokl."

"But, but . . ." I stuttered, "but I thought you were Larry's campaign manager."

"I am."

"And you said he's the best man for the job. . . ."

"Sure he is. But *she's* a girl!"

IN THE FIELD of comedy, Bob Hope's most precious possessions are called "one liners." They're terse, pithy sentences that get the build-up and punch line condensed into one devastating sentence. Children, by their very directness, are masters of the one-line delivery. Here's a choice collection of bombs:

Did you see Santa this year?
See him? I fixed him a bourbon and water.

◆ ◆ ◆

If you could change school any way you wished, how would you fix it?
Burn it down.

◆ ◆ ◆

What's your best subject in school?
Recess.

◆ ◆ ◆

What are muscles?
  Sick meatballs.

◆ ◆ ◆

Have any brothers?
  I have two.
What ages?
  Ricky's two months, and David's nine months.
That's a pretty fast production record . . . do you want a sister?
  Yes.
What does your mother say?
  She says, "Oh, puh-leeze, no!"

◆ ◆ ◆

Any brothers or sisters?
  No, but I've got an idea how to get one.
How?
  Well, I'm going to give Mommy a lot of real sweet food so she'll get fat—that's how you get a baby.

◆ ◆ ◆

Do you have any brothers or sisters?
  No.
Any plans for any?
  We're going to have a baby brother.
How do you know?
  My dad told me.
What about your mother?

He hasn't told her yet; we're keeping it a secret.

◆ ◆ ◆

Who does your baby sister look like?
    My mother.
And your oldest sister?
    My father.
And you?
    The mailman.
How so?
    That's what my mother is always telling the neighbors.

◆ ◆ ◆

What do you want to be?
    A nurse.
What if I came in with a headache?
    I'd put a wet rag on your head.
What if I had a stomachache?
    I'd tell you you were having a baby. That would scare you!
It sure would.

◆ ◆ ◆

Do you want to be a bachelor?
    No.
Why not?
    Because my dad's a bachelor.

◆ ◆ ◆

What are you interested in becoming?

A movie star like Marilyn Monroe.
Why?
I like the way she walks.

◆ ◆ ◆

What would you like to be?
A movie star like Liz Taylor so I could wear those strapless, backless and frontless dresses.

◆ ◆ ◆

Do you have any pets?
A cat.
What's his name?
We're going to change it because he's a boy cat and next week he's going to have an operation and become an "it."
What will you call him then?
Christine.
If he doesn't like that, you can call him Sam Spade!

◆ ◆ ◆

What will you be when you grow up?
A nurse or a veterinarian or an airline stewardess.
Why that category?
Because I like animals and men.

THE PRESENCE or absence of the subject under discussion is no deterrent in the mind of a child. He would not soften the blow or exaggerate the compliment just because the person being talked about is there. If you want his opinion, you're going to get it. And sometimes, when you *don't* want it, he'll toss it your way blithely. One day when I was asking the common question: "What would you like to be?" a young man looked me right in the eye and clearly stated: "Well, this job of yours looks pretty soft to me."

Another five year old said he'd like to be a fireman and rescue people from burning buildings. When I asked him if he'd like to rescue me, he scoffed and said:

"Heck no. I'm lookin' for ladies in their nightgowns!"

Another older child was explaining the mysteries of playground slang:

"Then we say: 'dig that crazy prehistoric.' "

"What's a 'prehistoric'?" I naively inquired.

"Anybody that's real old. Like you!"

A six year old sweetheart had told me she dearly desired to be a lady doctor.

"Who would be your patients?"

"Tony Curtis, Gene Autry, Roy Rogers and Art Linkletter," she rattled off.

"Why all men?"

"I like men," she flirted mischievously.

"I wonder what you'd do for all of us?" I went on.

"Well, I don't know what I'd do for the rest of them. But," and she surveyed me judiciously, "the first thing I'd do for you would be to put you on a diet."

LITTLE GIRLS, with curly locks, pink bows, and angel eyes, can be just as devastating as boys any day in the week, and perhaps double on Sundays. Their soft little mouths and turned up noses mask an artless approach that leaves victims strewn on the conversational battlefield as far as the eye can see. Here are two examples:

"So you'd like to be a private secretary, Jane. Would you like to work for me?"

"Gosh, no!"

"Why not?"

"Because I want to work for a gentleman!"

I didn't have the courage to ask her what she thought I was. I went on to Kathleen:

"How old are you, darling?"

"Six."

"My, my . . . are those bags under your eyes?"

"Yes. I didn't get to sleep till 8:30 last night."

"Well, that's terrible to have those bags."

"*You* have them, too, Mr. Linkletter. Only *yours* are *bigger!*"

If you can't stand this kind of repartee, my suggestion is to run, don't walk, to the nearest exit when a child approaches. But you'd be amazed at how warm and human you begin to feel after the first few shocks. You'll be tempted to yell to timid souls outside the circle of tiny friends, "Come on in, the candor's fine!"

THE KIDS ARE just as frank about themselves. They'll admit to intimate frailties that can't be torn from them by brainwashing ten years hence. One morning recently I said:

"What did you do to get ready for today's show?"

"I was in such a hurry I got my pants on backwards," the young lady giggled.

Sternly kidding, I said: "Don't you know that we don't allow little girls on this show with their pants on backwards?"

"Oh, it's all right now," she assured me. "I went to the bathroom and put the back that was in the front in the back."

Another young guest said: "I want to be anything but what you are."

"What's so bad about my job?"

"You have to put up with kids like me every day."

A young fellow was wearing both suspenders and belt to the program. When I inquired why, he stated forthrightly:

"Because if my pants fell down I'd have to run home and I wouldn't get a prize."

When I complimented a beautifully dressed young lady on her appearance, she proudly told me that she was wearing a dress and two slips.

"Why *two* slips?" I asked.

"Because the pretty one itches."

Then there was the delightful seven-word sentence that so aptly answered my question:

"What's new with you, little girl?"

"My pink pants with the blue bows."

The open heart of a trusting child is spread out before you with those words. Cutting across artificial rules of expression and behavior, she says simply and unabashedly what gladdens her life at that precise moment.

Chapter 7

Just Plain Fun

"IF I could have a wish, I wish I had a giant chicken so big it could hatch the world."

A five year old is talking. He's playing the favorite game of children of all ages. He's pretending something that's delightful, amusing or gratifying. He's using the part of his mind that produces poets, inventors, painters, musicians and daydreamers. He is learning to live within himself.

Through the years, I've devoted a large part of my time on the air to talking with children about the "pretend" part of their thinking. I've asked them to divulge their innermost wish, to tell us what kind of an animal they'd like to be; to reveal where they'd like to travel, to explain their favorite fun and to announce what age they'd prefer to be and why. As you might expect, their answers are surprising, and their reasoning even more so.

"Are you having a good time today?"

"Oh, yes sir," replied a seven year old joy-fully. "This is lots of fun."

121

"What do you like best about TV City: the cameras, the stages, the lights?"

"I like the blonde at the front desk."

An older child with experience in the pitfalls of an educational career announced:

"If I could invent anything, I'd make some glasses with open eyeballs painted on them so you could sit in class and sleep and the teacher would think you were listening."

An even craftier lad had a devious reason for wishing to be a snake. He explained:

"Because if you poison people and you're a person they put you in jail. But they couldn't put you in there if you're a snake because there aren't any snake jails!"

THE FOUR YEAR olds are completely delightful in their artless response to "if you could be" questions. Here are a few samples that no grown-up could ever invent:

◆ "I'd like to be a fish 'cause I like to wag my tail when I take a bath."

◆ "I'd like to be six. I'm tired of being five. I've been five for a whole year."

◆ "I'd like to be growed up. I want to see what it's like."

◆ "I like to play Army, but I'm getting tired of it. I'm always the enemy."

◆ "I'd like to be forty-five so I could watch TV until thirty o'clock at night."

IF ALL ELSE fails, here is the question that opens the conversational floodgates of the kids: "What do you like to do best?" Some of the imaginative rejoinders are based on fact, but many venture forth into the great field of make-believe where Peter Pan beckons. Here's a boy who is *almost* a successful inventor:

"I'm building a funny machine in my backyard so I can play jokes on people."

"How does it work?"

"There's a wire that trips them and they fall down and are carried down a big moving belt that finally drops them into a black hole where I take all their money."

Another little dreamer had an even more fantastic pastime . . . if you believe this:

"I like to jump on my pogo stick and bounce right up to heaven."

"What do you see up there?"

"Girl angels, dog angels, cat angels and fish angels."

"No *boy* angels?" I protested.

"No. Boy angels and worm angels don't go to heaven."

PURE, JOYOUS, untrammeled ignorance is the basis for an average five year old's concept of the world. Unfettered by fact, and flying free on the updraft of his dreams, he explores every bizarre corner of the universe.

"This summer I'm going to the bottom of the world to see what it would be like if you fell off."

Calmly accepting this preposterous statement as fact, I gravely posed this question:

"And where, do you suppose, is the bottom of the world?"

"Oh, it's a long way off. Texas, I think."

Another global adventurer had plans for an even more unusual trip: "I'm going to Las Vegas where I can see the alligators and bears and the Statue of Liberty."

There may be more truth buried in that sentence than first meets the eye. I have grown-up friends who have come back from a Las Vegas weekend with sillier stories than that.

"I'D LIKE TO go to Utah," wished a young man.

"Why Utah?"

"I want to see the California seagulls."

"What would California seagulls be doing in Utah?"

"They went up there to eat the Mormons and get out of the smog."

And here's a whimsical wish that no one could be blamed for thinking:

"I want to go to Missouri because I've always wanted to see the Missouri waltz."

THE "CONFUSED SET" takes over when the four year olds arrive on the scene:

"I want to go to Florida to see the roof tops fly off."

"What makes you think this happens?"

"Everybody's heard of the terrible earthquakes they have there."

◆ I want to go to New York to see the cow-boys and Indians kill each other. (This boy must mean the Yankees and the Indians.)

◆ I want to go to Kansas because that's where my mother and daddy are going to get married sometime.

◆ I want to go downtown.
What's the first thing you'd do if you got lost downtown?
   Holler!

EVEN THE LITTLE ones have become in-fected with the Washington "gimmee" dis-ease that has proved so contagious. Listen to this tiny lobbyist:
   "I want to go to Washington, D. C."
   "Who do you want to see?"
   "Either President Abraham Lincoln or President Carter."
   "Well, it might be easier to see Jimmy than Abe. What would you talk about?"
   "He's a nice man, and I think he would give us a new house for the family if I asked him polite."
   Here's a daydream that must have blitzed them at the next faculty meeting:
   "What animal would you like to be, Bobby?"
   "A big mean lion."
   "Why?"
   "So I could scare everybody."
   "Even your teacher?"
   "Heck no. *Nothing* could scare *her*."

AND NOW let's look over a few choice comments by the children on the subject of "age." Almost everyone alive is dissatisfied with his status when it comes to age. We all wish we were younger or older, for a variety of reasons. Children have startling reasons of their own:

What age would you like to be instead of six?

Seventeen, 'cause then you're an old woman and pretty soon you'll be with God.

◆ ◆ ◆

You're five. How old would you like to be?

Fourteen.

Why?

So I can be a father. (He paused to consider.) I'd like to start with fifty-one children.

◆ ◆ ◆

How old are you?

Six and three quarters and a half.

And how old would you like to be?

The oldest man in the world.

What gave you that idea?

Because then my name would be in the Bible and if I'd been good I'd be the highest in heaven, and if I'd been bad I'd be the lowest on earth.

◆ ◆ ◆

I'd like to stay eleven, because then I'd never have to know the facts of life.

◆ ◆ ◆

I'd like to stay eleven forever, because the minute you're twelve you have to pay more for everything.

◆ ◆ ◆

I'd like to be twelve so I could marry Casey and have some children.
How many?
Three of each kind as a start.
How will Casey make a living for this big family?
That's not *my* worry. *He's* got to think of something.

◆ ◆ ◆

How old are you?
Seven.
How old would you like to be?
Nine.
Why?
It's more peaceful.

◆ ◆ ◆

I'd like to be twenty-one so I could join the Army.
Which branch do you like?
The Marines.
Who would you fight?
The Germans.
We're not fighting them this year.
Then, the Japs.
Why, that war's all over, too.

I don't worry. By the time I'm twenty-one, there'll be *someone* to fight.

◆   ◆   ◆

I like being eleven.
What's so good about being eleven?
Your stomach is larger than before and you can eat more.

◆   ◆   ◆

What's the best part of being ten?
My allowance is bigger.
How much do you get?
Fifty cents.
How much did you get before?
Seventy-five cents.
Whoa! You're going the wrong way, aren't you? Isn't that smaller?
My sister got married last January and my folks are still broke.

◆   ◆   ◆

How old are you?
Six.

How old would you like to be?

Seven.

Why?

Because when you're seven you can be a Hawaiian.

THE DIFFERENCE between a six year old and a twelve year old girl is forcefully under-scored in this conversation with the younger set:

"What did you do at your birthday party that was interesting?"

"We played post office for a while, but we quit."

"Why did you stop?"

"It isn't any fun. It's just a lot of old kissing and mushy stuff and nobody likes that."

The older set has a game that's a little more advanced called "monster." An eleven year old girl explained how it's played:

"Well, the girls are monsters and the boys have to catch them."

"Then what happens?"

"Then they let them go and try to catch them again."

"Do you think you'll be a 'monster' when you grow up?" I teased her.

"No, I'd rather be Marilyn Monroe because then they never let you go."

NOT ALL girls want to be an actress when they grow up. Here are some other career ideas advanced by the kids:

What will you be?
   A nurse.
What if you had a handsome, romantic patient?
   I'd read to him.
And if you had a crabby, old, ugly one?
   I'd give him sleeping pills.

◆ ◆ ◆

What would you like to be?
   A stewardess.
What if a plane was in danger over the Rocky Mountains?
   I'd put parachutes on everybody and if there wasn't any parachutes I'd sew up sheets into parachutes real fast and put in extra pillows so if the sheets ripped on the way down, they could always land on the pillows.

◆ ◆ ◆

What do you want to be?
   A fireman.

What would you do if there were a fire on the fourth floor of a hotel and you had to get a great, fat lady down?

I'd get a gun with a rope on it and shoot it up to her and she could tie it around her waist and jump out.

◆　◆　◆

What would you like to be?

A bluebird.

Why?

So I could eat worms.

Why do you think you'd like them?

Because birds like them.

What would you guess they taste like?

Kind of like an ordinary, average worm tastes.

◆　◆　◆

What animal wouldn't you like to be?

A lion or a tiger.

Why?

They eat people and people don't taste so good.

◆　◆　◆

If you were President of the U.S. how would you change the country?

I'd change television so all the good shows that are on late would be on early.

◆　◆　◆

What type boy are you?

I'm a dreamer.

What kind of dreamer?

Well, I have daydreams in the daytime about going to the moon, and at night I just dream about girls.

How will you be a better boy this year?

I'm not going to fight, or if I do, I won't take the first lick, just the last one.

What do you want to be?

An evangelist like Billy Graham.

What's the most important part of being an evangelist?

Getting a big collection.

Who're smarter—boys or girls?

Girls are smarter in school, but it's for a reason.

What's the reason?

They cheat.

◆ ◆ ◆

What do you want to be?

A teacher.

What would you do with bad boys and girls?

Put them in a thinking chair and let them think about how bad they've been.

What if the whole class were bad?
I'd tie them all up and roll them in a corner.

◆ ◆ ◆

What are you going to be?
A train engineer.
What's the main thing to remember about being an engineer?
Not to drive the train off the tracks.

◆ ◆ ◆

What did you do to get ready today?
Stuck on my old clothes.

◆ ◆ ◆

Any hobbies?
I collect all kinds of stuff: cards, matches, rocks, automobiles, hats.
What are you going to be when you grow up?
A junkman.

◆ ◆ ◆

What do you want to be?
   A traffic officer.
What if you caught Marilyn Monroe speeding?
   I'd kiss her first then arrest her.

◆ ◆ ◆

What do you want to be?
   A baby nurse.
What would you do if a baby had a pain in the big toe?
   Hang her up on the clothesline.

◆ ◆ ◆

What do you want to be?
   A nurse.
What if I came in with a broken arm?
   I'd sew it on.
Broken head?
   Sew it on.
Broken leg?
   I'd sew it on.

◆ ◆ ◆

What are you going to be?
   A nurse, to help sick people.
What if I had a headache?
   I'd give you a Bufferin.
Stomachache?
   Ginger ale.
Arthritis?
   Carter's Little Liver Pills.
What about a bad cold?
   Bottle of Eastside Beer.

I BELIEVE THAT the "imagery muscles" of a child's mind can be exercised and developed in the same way that his biceps are built. He must use them frequently and to the limit before any real growth can be expected, and he must "want" to stretch them. In the Linkletter family we attempted this through games in which we made up "whoppers" and tried to leave the story dangling in some impossible crisis for the next narrator to solve. Aviators, with ticking bombs manacled to their body, float earthward from burning airplanes with starving moths eating the parachute silk, while below him is an endless vista of gaping crocodile jaws in the quicksands of the jungle. This sort of "cliff-hanger" is calculated to improve the imagination, quicken the mind, and get the growing child to bed with a head start on a rip snorting nightmare.

But it was fun for the family, and I transferred the Linkletter bedtime formula to the television show with considerable success. It worked perfectly—up to a point — with a young sailor boy, resplendent in full maritime regalia designed for six year olds.

"You must be an admiral," I began admiringly.

"Better'n that," he corrected. "I'm a bosun's mate."

"How do you know?"

"My dad told me. He was a bosun's mate."

"Oh!" I couldn't correct an authority like *that*. "What else do you know about the Navy?"

"Almost everything."

"All right then, suppose you were captain of a ship away out in the ocean and it was sinking with a big hole in the bottom. What would you do?"

"I'd put on a big diving suit with muscles, and dive in the water and hold it up until it could be fixed."

"What if the ship were burning?"

"I'd grab a hose, start the pumps and put it out."

"What if you ran into an iceberg and a lot of polar bears came aboard?"

"I'd get a knife and cut their throats."

"Well, then, suppose there was a bomb on board and you didn't know where it was hidden?"

"I'd search all over and find it and throw it away."

"And if you *didn't* find it?"

"Well, I guess I'd be done for and go down with the ship."

He was through with the game and made no bones about it. That's part of the fun. When the mental "hide and go seek" is over, everyone's supposed to give up and come back to home base so the next game can start. If you don't believe me, try to prolong a game of any kind once the child is ready to quit.

SPEAKING OF games, I love the way the younger children are resigned to their lot when it comes to organizing the fun. One five year old told me he enjoyed "hide and seek."

"How do you play it?"

"I cover my eyes and all the big boys go and hide someplace."

"Where do you hide when it's not your turn to be 'it'?"

"I don't know. I'm always 'it.'"

The best games are the ones where the kids pretend to be grown-ups. No girl has ever enjoyed a normal childhood who has not dressed up in her mother's high heeled shoes, fancy hat and long dress, and gone flopping around the house pretending she's adult.

"How do you like to play house?" I asked a five year old miss.

"I fix dinner for my husband and ten children," she gravely responded.

"Do you do plain or fancy cooking?"

"Mostly I fry the chicken and fix the 'taters and gravy."

"Do you know what you do first to fry chicken?"

"Yep. You kill it. Then you peel it."

DOLLS, OF COURSE, afford a little girl glowing opportunities to play "mother." The poorest child is rich if she has a doll to cuddle and love at night. One girl even boasted:

"My doll is the best doll because she does most things by herself."

"Like what?"

"Well, she snores by herself, and at night

kneels down by the bed and prays. And she
drinks and goes to the bathroom all by herself."

"That sounds like a pretty wonderful doll
all right," I conceded. "Did you say it does
this *all* by itself?"

"Well, I help it a little."

And from this charming make-believe with
the gravely serious little "parent," we come
to the sister who takes care of her problems
in a different mood.

"I like to put on plays."

"What's your favorite?"

"One where I'm queen and my sister is a
princess and anybody who shakes hands with
her is killed."

"Well, who shakes hands with her in the
play?"

"All the kids in the neighborhood."

"How does the play end?"

"I shake hands with her, but *she* dies instead of me."

BOYS, NO LESS than girls, are full of in-
genuity when play time arrives. Their pleasure is apt to be a trifle bloodthirsty as they
grow older, but at five or six they are satisfied with peaceful pursuits. One young man
had a game called "soda fountain."

"How do you play it?"

"I pretend a customer comes up and asks
for a steak, salad, and orange juice."

"Do you give it to him?"

"Sure."

"Do you *have* all of this stuff at the fountain?"

"No."

"Then how do you give it to him?"

"He's just a make-believe customer, like
my food." He grinned in complete satisfaction.

Only one thing a young man hates more
than all that mushy kissing stuff with girls is
what happened to young Donald. He
explained:

"We played post office at this party."

"That sounds exciting. Did you enjoy it?"

"Not the way we played it."

"What happened?"

"I got a wrong letter and had to kiss
another boy!"

At one of my own children's birthday parties a young guest surreptitiously gave me
the high sign. He had an ominous tone in
his voice as I bent over to hear the whispered confidence. Through his lisps, I
gathered that an imposter had wormed his
way into the happy group.

"Mr. Linkletter. You know that clown who's playing all the games with us?"

"Of course," I replied. I knew the clown extremely well because he was the famous Pinto Colvig of Walt Disney's studios, who had come over in his full make-up to help out with the fun.

"He's not a *real* clown!" He stopped to gulp, overcome with excitement. "I've been watching him. And he took off those white gloves. And Mr. Linkletter, *he has skin just like the rest of us.*"

The significance of this pronouncement took a moment to sink in, and then I realized how seriously the little folks take the subject of organized fun. A clown is someone born for just that occupation, red nose, big mouth and flat feet!

OF COURSE, some children grow up much faster than others. They disdain juvenile pursuits almost before they know what they are. Here's a prime example:

"I'm going to be six tomorrow."

"Going to have a birthday party?"

"Naw."

"You're *not*? Why not? Don't you *like* parties?"

"I don't like all those little kids around. There's too much disturbance."

The really older boys, who have attained the advanced rank of ten year olds, graduate to more sophisticated fun. One of these youngsters told me he played a game called "Recess."

"I've never heard of a *game* called 'Recess,'" I commented. "How's it played?"

"The main thing is to try to get out of going to school."

"You mean, you want a permanent, ever-lasting recess?"

"That's right."

"Have you had any success?"

"Not so far this year. But I had a great year last year!" He smiled blissfully.

"How do you mean?"

"Well I had three earaches, tonsillitis, sinus trouble, the mumps, and finally I got a shot. That's the end." He blushed suddenly and corrected himself. "I mean, that's the end of the *story*."

Another lad assured me that the old game of Cowboys and Indians was still the best.

"Which one are you?"

"I like to be an Indian 'cause we always scalp the cowboys."

"You don't *really* scalp them, do you?" I scoffed.

"Sure. We just take a big knife and cut his hair off."

"What do you do with the hair?"

"We give it to one of the bald-headed Indians."

And that explains the mystery of what became of all that pioneer hair from your forefathers! But, speaking of scalping, here is a modern version played by a smart father:

"What sort of games do you play?"

"Oh, I play card games with my dad."

"What kind of card games?"

"For a quarter."

"Why a quarter?"

"Because that's my allowance. We play till he wins it, and then we quit."

Chapter 8

Little Faces Looking Up

EVERY minute of every hour a child is soaking up information—whether it's a new word, a new thought or the knowledge that when you sock somebody in the nose he's very likely to poke you back. Some of this avalanche of learning comes through clear and loud, while other tidbits are like a picture slightly out of focus. You see it and hear it, but it doesn't *quite* make sense.

Years ago, before the Pledge of Allegiance was changed, I heard a youngster solemnly repeat: "I pledge allegiance to the Flag of the United States, and to the Republic for which it stands. One naked individual with liberty and justice for all."

Half-heard, and half-understood, words and phrases project a kaleidoscopic pattern of life on the nerve endings of a growing child. His memory processes are baffled by the continuing barrage of new sounds, and when he strikes out through the dense undergrowth of the English language, some amusing adventures in semantics result.

One of my all-time favorites is the boy who said: "My favorite song is 'I'm going to Alabama with a band-aid on my knee.'"

A little girl came to a costume party at the Linkletter house one day wearing a fancy colonial costume. "Who are you supposed to be?" I wondered.

"I'm George Washington's wife. She saved her father's life by jumping on a horse and riding through the town yelling 'The British are coming.'"

Listen carefully sometime to a group of youngsters singing a standard song, and you'll be convulsed by the phrases they unconsciously mangle. A small friend of ours when singing "God Bless America" comes out with the logical lyrics: "Stand beside her, and guide her, with the light through the night from a bulb."

AFTER ALL THESE years around children, my ears are tuned for these priceless misstatements. They reflect the frantic efforts of tiny nervous systems to assimilate the constant stream of random information. When it's played back, sometimes the needle jumps the groove and we marvel at the malapropisms that result.

I guess you might call me an amateur child psychologist. I've studied the subject in college, read books by leading experts and spent many hours discussing children with the top people in the field. But my only real claim to knowledge about kids is in my day by day contacts. The only way to know about children is to be with them. And five of my own youngsters who grew up around me seven days a week for twenty years attest to my veteran standing in the profession.

It seems impossible that once upon a time I was as naive about parenthood as the young husband who solicitously asked his pregnant bride on the way to the hospital:

"Darling, are you *sure* you want to go through with this?"

And yet, there has to be a beginning. With me, it was a blond, wiggling, red-faced boy named Jack. Weight at birth, 9 pounds 6 ounces; length, 22 inches. As he grew up he was not particularly naughty or disobedient, or destructive or defiant. He was simply omnivorous and about as discriminating as a garbage disposal unit. Spankings were absorbed with hardly a blink, and he was eternally optimistic about not getting caught the next time. I developed the habit of spanking him first thing when I got home from work, on the practical theory that if *I* didn't know what he'd been doing wrong, *he* would!

Today, at 6 feet, 3 inches, he has survived the rigors of growing up, and is about to learn for himself why an exasperated father was once heard to say: "I just want to live long enough to be as much of a nuisance to my children as they've been to me!"

Somebody once said that the reason God chose young people to repopulate the earth is because they have the stamina to endure close contact with little children. Yes, children are adorable, but it takes real staying power to handle their driving curiosity and perpetual motion twenty-four hours a day.

Every one of our five children is an individual person who might have been dropped into our family circle from some different set of parents. The thought of one general set of rules applying to all of them is an absurdity. Punishments, rewards, and incentives vary widely in their effectiveness, depending on *which* child and *what* circumstance.

The really important rule in bringing up children is to train them lovingly, demand their obedience, and don't frustrate them unnecessarily. What really matters is the relationship between the child and his parents. It is how we feel deep down in our hearts toward our children that really counts. A child will endure pain, disappointments, and even fear if he is loved. And his intuitive perception cannot be fooled. Training by love is a quick way to say it.

STILL, EVEN the most conscientious instruction "jumps the rails" often enough to give us a joyous glimpse into the struggling young faces looking up at us for learning. Here are some of my best recollections:

What does it mean to have patience? Can you give us some examples?

◆ A hundred year jail sentence.

◆ An old maid waiting to get married.

◆ Waiting for Mother to finish "grace" while the supper gets cold.

◆ Waiting in the comfort station for the guy ahead of you to finish.

◆   ◆   ◆

What does it mean when you say that something is just "horse sense?"

Well, people can spend money . . . but horses can't because they haven't any cents.

◆   ◆   ◆

Who knows what "failure" means?

When you have your eye on some real cute boy at school and by the time you get all cooked up about him, some other girl grabs him.

◆   ◆   ◆

I'm glad to see someone whose teeth are so white and shining. Do you brush yours three times every day?

No, sir. Just once. But I use Clorox.

◆   ◆   ◆

What's the funniest thing that ever happened to you?

I came back from the bathroom one day at school. Suddenly, I noticed that my zipper was undone and I said to myself, "I'm insulting my own inheritance."

Why are you wearing a bow tie today?

It's the only way I can think of to show people I'm really a man.

What's the hardest table manners for you to remember?

To remember to swallow after I take a drink of milk before I start talking.

Do you have any difficulty about remembering to use a napkin?

We never have them at our table. We lick.

Have you ever been spanked? What for?

At my uncle's farm house I was watching the pigs in the pig pen, and they looked like they were having so much fun, I did it.

I hope you know how to handle money. Do you have any?

No. I had six cents but I gave it to my girl friend.

Does she still have it?

Oh, no. This was a month ago. I'll bet she's spent all of it.

What are you learning at school that you can tell us about?

They teach you not to fight with your friends.

How do they do that?

They read from the Bible, where Jesus says, "Thou shalt not kill."

I'm happy to learn that they've stopped the killing on the playgrounds this way. But tell me, have you been punished lately?

Yes.

What for?

Hitting a kid in the face with a cupcake.

Why did you do that?

It's not in the Bible.

◆　◆　◆

You look like Toothless Joe to me. How many of those teeth are you missing?

Five so far, but two more are ready.

That must be terrible.

Oh, no. It's good. I don't have to eat anything I don't like. And when they *all* fall out, I'll just eat ice cream the rest of my life. (He grinned happily.) I *like* ice cream.

◆　◆　◆

I'm learning to catch bees. We'll have all the honey we want for pancakes.

That's a perfect way to make a hobby pay off. How do you catch bees?

I wait till they light on a floor, then I run up behind them with a glass jar, and the silly bee thinks the bottom of the jar is the top but it's really the bottom 'cause it's upside down and the top is on the bottom, and the bee gets all mixed up.

I know just how the bee feels!

◆ ◆ ◆

What are good manners to remember at lunch to-day?

Don't throw up on the table.

◆ ◆ ◆

How old are you?

Five years old.

I can't hear you. Are you losing your voice?

Yes. I went to bed without my pajama bottoms and woke up without my voice.

What are you doing for it?

I take a little lemon and honey and bour-bon.

◆ ◆ ◆

What do you think a rich man is?
   A bachelor.

◆   ◆   ◆

How do you know when you're in love?
   You hear bells.
And if you're not?
   You hear sirens.

◆   ◆   ◆

How do you get money?
   I get a nickel every day I don't have a damp bed.
How are you doing?
   I made a dime last week.

◆   ◆   ◆

I see that you have a tooth missing.
   Two of them. And the Good Fairy brought me $2.00.
Did you see what she looked like?
   Yes, she had two arms, two legs, one head, a moustache and she was wearing pajama tops.

◆   ◆   ◆

   I'm going to be an airline hostess, because you get to meet movie stars and millionaires.
How do you know?
   Because I have an aunt who was one and she had dates with 'em all.
Then what happened?
   She married a Marine.

◆　◆　◆

How do you know when you're in love?

I never knew what it was like until I was eight.

How old are you now?

Twelve.

Tell us what happened.

My sister fixed up a blind date. We went together for two years. Then, she quit me when I was ten, and my heart failed.

◆　◆　◆

How do you know when you're in love?

They start biting their nails, then they fall down in pieces, and start crying and can't stop.

◆　◆　◆

I want to be a parachute jumper.

What happens if your parachute won't open?

I have them lower a ladder.

◆　◆　◆

I want to be a nurse and mix up stuff for people.

What would you mix up for me if I had a tummy ache?

A bottle of milk of magnesia and a bottle of castor oil ought to do something.

◆　◆　◆

Do you have a philosophy of life?
  Don't goof off.
Would you explain that expression in English?
  Don't mess around. Don't flub up.

◆ ◆ ◆

Do you know when George Washington was born?
  In 1732 in Kentucky, California.
Where is that?
  It's in Tennessee.
What's Washington famous for?
  The one-dollar bill.

◆ ◆ ◆

  I'm going to be a scientist and study bones.
Then you must know what a dinosaur is?
  Yes, it's a place where you buy things for five and ten cents.

◆ ◆ ◆

  I want to be an actress like Jack Benny.

◆ ◆ ◆

  I think one of the best inventions was the Morse code but I don't know the name of the man that invented it.

◆ ◆ ◆

Do you have a pet?
  A dog.
Does he have a pedigree?

Sure, lot of them.
How do you know?
Because he bites himself all the time.

◆   ◆   ◆

What is an optimist?
The opposite of peptomist.

◆   ◆   ◆

What's your favorite food?
Shwimp.
How do you like it cooked?
Fwied.

◆   ◆   ◆

Would you vote for a woman for president?
No.
Why not?
Their responsibilities aren't so political.

◆   ◆   ◆

What do you want to be when you grow up?
Nothing, because I don't want to grow up.
That's unusual. How come?
Because of all the bills you have to pay at the end of the month.

◆   ◆   ◆

What do you want to be:
I want to follow in my dad's footsteps.
What is he?
I don't know.

◆ ◆ ◆

What do you want to be?
  A nurse in a maternity hospital.
Who gave you that idea?
  Nobody. I just like babies.
What would you do with a screaming, whimper-ing, crying, kicking baby?
  That's easy; I'd leave it alone.

◆ ◆ ◆

Who matures faster, girls or boys?
  Girls.
How do you know?
  Well, a girl knows when she falls in love with a boy but a boy doesn't even know that the girl's in love with him or what, and doesn't know much of anything—so girls are more mature.

◆ ◆ ◆

How do you get money?
  I don't—that's why I'm so desperate for some.
What do you think you'll be when you grow up?
  A fortune hunter and find a millionaire.

How will you find him?
  Somewhere—and I'll get a stranglehold on him.

◆ ◆ ◆

What do you have to find out about a man before marrying him?
  His address and phone number.
Who are you going to marry?
  Bruce.
Known him long?
  Since yesterday.

◆ ◆ ◆

If you had one wish what would it be?
  I'd like to have the war ended.
That's a very praiseworthy wish, but I'm in doubt . . . which war do you mean?
  The Civil War.

◆ ◆ ◆

How old are you, Darrell?
  Ten and three-quarters.
What's your philosophy of life?
  I'm optimistic about life but pessimistic about girls.
How so?
  Well, I have a dim look of them.

◆ ◆ ◆

Would you like to be the President?
  Oh, it's all right.
The Governor?

No . . . not 'specially.
How about the mayor?
No!
Why not?
Because that's a girl horse.

◆ ◆ ◆

What do you like to do best?
Cook, sew, embroider, and clean house.
With those interests, what do you think you'll be?
A private secretary.
Do you know what a private secretary does?
Yes, the main thing is to keep the news-papermen away from her boss so they can't get a scoop on anything he doesn't want them to know about.
Would you be willing to sit on the boss' lap?
Well, if you have to—you have to!

◆ ◆ ◆

Let's talk about table manners. Every little boy and girl is judged by the way he acts at the table. Who can think of some bad manners to watch out for?

◆ Don't throw food under the table if there's not a dog under there, because it'll rot.

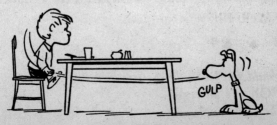

◆ You should always turn your head when you sneeze at the table, but you'd better grab your plate and take it with you, because then people can't sneak vegetables on your plate that you don't want while your head's turned.

◆ Don't talk with your mouth full 'cause you might choke to death.

◆ Never throw pies in the company's face.

◆ Don't use your dress for a napkin when your mother's looking.

◆ Ask for extra helpings instead of scraping the bottom of the plate till all the picture's worn off.

◆ Don't put your food in other people's drinks.

◆ ◆ ◆

What do you want to be?
　I don't care as long as I get money.
Why do you want money?
　Because I want to have a husband and the only way you can get a husband these days is to have money.

◆ ◆ ◆◆

You're from Virginia . . . what's that state famous for?

For one thing, George Washington was born there, and then there's Thomas Jefferson who wrote the Declaration of Independence; he lives right up the hill from me.

◆　◆　◆

Do you know anything about the Irish?
    I know what a leprechaun is.
What is it?
    It's a terrible disease where your skin falls off.

◆　◆　◆

What's the most important thing in a girl's life?
    Makeup and men.
What's most important in a man's life?
    Money, money, money and Marilyn Monroe.

◆　◆　◆

Have any hobbies?
    I used to be the junk collector around my house.
What happened?
    One day my dad told me to sort everything alphabetically and I didn't know what he meant . . . I thought he was telling me to throw everything out and now I haven't got a hobby.

◆　◆　◆

What kind of boy are you?

A serious boy.
Well, then let's talk about something serious. What do you think of world affairs and the United Nations?
Is *that* serious?

◆ ◆ ◆

What do you want to be?
I'm not sure but I think I'd like to get married.
Why?
Well, I'd rather do that than work.

◆ ◆ ◆

What do you want to be?
Housewife.
Who are you going to marry?
I think a woman.
But you're a girl yourself . . . why do you want to marry a woman?
Because women are a lot less trouble than men, my mother tells me.

◆ ◆ ◆

What do you want to be?
A Marine.
Why?
I like the hats.
Any other reason?
I want to help the Navy fight the Army.

◆ ◆ ◆

What do you want to be?

A children's dentist.

Why?

Because I'll drill better.

What don't you like about the present way of drilling?

It hurts.

What will you do to help that?

I'll pull the teeth out, then they won't have to be drilled.

◆ ◆ ◆

What do you want to be?

A producer.

What makes you want to be that?

They have such an easy job.

What kind of a job do you think it is?

Well, the studio just sends them all the money they need and they just sit around with their feet on the desk and they talk to the reporters who come in and ask them questions about their next picture.

◆ ◆ ◆

What do you want to be?

An airline stewardess.

Why?

Because my mother was one and she married a millionaire.

Oh? What does your dad do?

He's a bartender.

What's your definition of "genius"?

◆ Someone who cheats and doesn't get caught.

◆ He's a fellow who gets into trouble; then some moron comes along and gets blamed.

◆ A genius is a man who wins an Emmy Award for being a great actor, like you.

◆ Someone who has wheels going around in his head all the time.

◆   ◆   ◆

What do you think an inferiority complex is?

◆ It's interference on a radar screen.

◆ It's a sort of disease you can catch if you're not careful.

◆   ◆   ◆

What do we mean by the expression "Man's best friend?"

◆ A TV set.

◆ Beer.

◆ A lady.

◆ A bed.

◆   ◆   ◆

Who would you change places with?
   Liberace.
Why?
   Because he has a nice swimming pool.
Well, he plays beautifully, too. And always has his candelabra with him. Do you know what candelabra is?
   Yes. I think it's a Spanish beer.

◆   ◆   ◆

Who would you like to be?
   Martha Washington.
Why?
   Because she married a millionaire and I'd like to do the same.
What else was Martha Washington famous for?
   For spending all her husband's money.
How do you know?
   I've seen pictures of him and he couldn't even afford a haircut. He wore a ponytail.

◆   ◆   ◆

Anything exciting happen today?
   On the way to the studio we saw a big restaurant on fire.
Who was there?
   Every fire department in town.

Who arrived last?
  The fire chief.
I wonder why?
  He probably took the long short-cut.

What do you think politics are?

◆ Another name for a horse trader.

◆ It's something you put in pillows.

◆ It's a thick book that's hard to read.

◆ It's kind of like a school where the teachers are real strick and there's bad boys in there.

How do you know when you're in love?

◆ When he puts his arm around you, you feel real cozy.

◆ You take her everywhere she wants to go and kiss her every night.

◆ You get goose pimples.

What's a gentleman?

◆ A man who doesn't talk too much.

◆ A man who pays for ladies' dinners.

◆ A man who fixes pipes for other people.

◆ A plain old man who's always polite.

◆ ◆ ◆

Why do men wear whiskers?

◆ So they can win contests.

◆ So that the ladies can tell them apart.

◆ To scare off bugs that light on their chin.

◆ So they can tickle little boys and girls.

◆ ◆ ◆

What's an adolescent?

◆ Somebody with pimples.

◆ Somebody who never stops talking.

◆ It's a kind of a commercial.

◆ He's crazy.

◆ ◆ ◆

What's a "good sport"?

A good sport is a guy who's no good at any kind of sport like tennis or football or swimming, so the only thing left for him is to be a good sport.

What's Armistice Day?
They have Armistice Day so boys and girls can go home from school and have a day of rest.

What does "the pitter-patter of tiny feet above" mean?
It means there's a leak in the roof and the rain's coming in.

What's your favorite slang expression?
"He's real stiggy boom."
What does it mean?
It can mean you're a real cool, nice fellow, or else it can mean you're a bad guy.

What does it mean when we say "his bark is worse than his bite"?
It means that he talks a lot and everybody knows he's stupid.

What's matrimony?
◆ I think it's something to play with. (Tommy, 5)

◆ It is something to eat? (Greta, 4½)

◆ It's a kind of medicine. (Helen, 6)

◆ It's a big stage. (Jackie, 5)

◆   ◆   ◆

What's the prettiest thing you ever saw?
  A bald-headed baby.

◆   ◆   ◆

Ever tried to cook?
  I tried to make some pancakes once.
What happened?
  Nothing much.
Why not?
  Because I left out the butter, milk, and eggs.

◆   ◆   ◆

What would you invent to help humanity?
  I'd invent a cookie-cleaner-upper.
Do you like cookies?
  Cookie's my parakeet.

What do you think of suspenders?
    I hate them.
Why?
    Because they get loose in back and fly up
and hit your head, boing!

What kind of name is your last one, "Sloma"?
    Bohemian.
Hungary?
    No, not yet. I had a late breakfast.

What's Abraham Lincoln famous for?

◆ He sailed around the world and discovered a
  new world called Los Angeles.

◆ He brought the states together and then
was finally shot while watching a movie.

◆ He was a famous sheriff who shot bad
men.

◆ He was a good President.
What was so good that he did?
    He grew a beard.

What's alimony?
    It's something Davey Crockett fought for
and finally lost.

◆ ◆ ◆

When will you reach maturity?
  I'll never get *there.*
Why not?
  Too far away.
What makes you think it's too far away?
  Well, isn't it an island in the South Pacific?

◆ ◆ ◆

What subject do you hate most?
  English.
Correct this sentence: If I'd a knew you was comin' I'd a baked a pie.
If I'd a knew you was comin' I'd a baked a cake.

◆ ◆ ◆

Easter morning is one of the most exciting times for a five year old, and I wonder if you can tell me what's the first thing you're going to do?
  Wake up.

Chapter 9

My Pet Pet Stories

ONCE upon a time, there were some mean and fearsome creatures known as Ogres. They lived in big castles, and made everybody miserable for miles around.

Then along came some Knights in shining armor who besieged the castles and clobbered every Ogre they could find. Unfortunately, a few Ogres escaped and are alive to this day. Maybe you've seen them yourself . . . they're the people who won't let kids have pets.

I believe all kids should have pets. It's an essential part of growing up. There's a mystic kinship between a boy and his dog, a sharing of love and trust that's unique. A boy's dog is his pal, his companion, his comforter when tears come, and his best listener to whispered secrets. At the price of a dog tag and a bowl of food each day, a pup's the biggest bargain in any kid's life.

Children love to talk about their pets, and with characteristic freedom, they weave many a fanciful tale of improbable goings on. If they don't have a pet, they blithely make one up.

One young man gravely assured me he had a pet . . . "A horse."

"Where does he live?" I asked.

"He sleeps with me."

"In the bedroom?"

"Yes."

I didn't want him to think I swallowed all this. That would be unfair to the Parents Union, so I asked if this was true.

"Of course!"

"What does he do when you go to school?"

"He gives free rides to my brother."

So I couldn't stump him. Who knows? Maybe he *does* sleep with a horse.

One boy had a ready answer when I asked what breed of dog he had:

"Half male and the other half airmale."

THE SUBJECT OF pedigrees is usually a challenging puzzler for the kids. They don't actually know what a pedigree is, but that doesn't stop them from using their imagination.

Like the time I asked a boy if he had any brothers or sisters.

"One brother, but he's a cat."

"What's his name?"

"Socrates."

"Does he have a pedigree?"

"No. It died last year."

Or this:

"You have a pet dog; is it pedigreed?"

"I think she lost her pedigreed last week."

One girl was sure her dog didn't have a pedigree. When I asked why, she said:

"Cause he's had his shots."

Perhaps the answer that brought the biggest laugh from our listeners on the fateful pedigree question was this exchange:

"Do you have any pets?"

"Yes—a cat and a dog."

"Do they have pedigrees?"

"No, we took them out!"

WHEN I WAS a kid I suppose we weren't very inventive about animals, because dogs were named "Rover" or "Prince," and cats were called "Pussy" or "Tabby." The modern generation has gone 'way beyond us with pet names.

"Do you have any pets?"

"I have a cat named Regal Pale."

"Why, that's the name of a beer company."

"No it isn't . . . it's the name of our cat. We had the cat before the beer company got its name, so they mus' have copied it from us."

If that kid's right, it must be a trend in the business. Come to think of it, I recall seeing another brand of beer around town called "Bull Dog."

Another little lady named her pet with admirable simplicity and logic.

"I have a pet cat we call Skunky."

"Why Skunky?"

"Because he's black and white all over— and he stinks!"

THE CONFUSION in little minds about the inevitable arrival of puppies and kittens leads to some intriguing replies.

When a girl told me about her cat, I asked her:

"Anything special about it?"

"No," said she. "So far she's just had 107 kittens."

(And who said it was rugged to lead a *dog's* life?)

Another girl, asked if she had any brothers or sisters, said she had something just as good.

"What's that?" I asked.

"A neighborhood cat."

"What's so good about that?"

"He runs around all the neighborhood having babies, and he's just making a fresh batch now!"

Then there was the girl who was befuddled about the sweet mysteries of life.

"Do you have any pets?"

"Yes—we have a dog that just laid six puppies."

SOME KIDS aren't content with the usual dog or cat. They branch out into menageries, like the boy who said:

"I have three guinea pigs, two dogs and a sick turkey."

"What's wrong with the turkey?"

"He's got the chicken pox."

One kid had a secret from his folks . . . but he told me:

"I'm keeping a hen under my bed in a box."

"What's it doing under there?"

"Well, I hope it's going to lay an egg, but so far, every time it gets ready to lay an egg, it runs over to the neighbor's yard and lays it there."

One of my favorites in the menagerie department is this one:

"I've got a dog—and I used to have chickens, ducks and rabbits."

"Where are the chickens, ducks and rabbits now?"

"In the freezer."

Ah, this cold, cold world!

TWO OF MY close friends in television are the Nelsons, and so it was with particular relish that I pulled this anecdote out of a young man one day:

Any pets?

I have two turtles named Ozzie and Harriet.

How can you tell which is which?

Don't you know? Ozzie is the *mean* one.

◆ ◆ ◆

I used to have a cat named Susie Q.

What happened to her?

It's a *him*.

A "him" named Susie Q? Well, anyway, what happened to him?

He was chasing a mouse and he ran into a tree and he was so ashamed he moved away.

◆ ◆ ◆

Have you any pets?

No.

Ever have any?

No.

Want any?

No.

Why not?

Because they make you scratch.

How do you know if you've never had a pet?

Because I had a friend who had a dog, and he gave the brother fleas, the daddy fleas, the mother fleas, and so then the baby got fleas and they all just sat around scratching.

◆ ◆ ◆

Every boy should own his own dog. Don't you agree?

I do. But my dad don't.

What does your dad think?

He doesn't think. He *knows*. Because we have a dog that bites.

What does it bite?

Mouses, cats, newspapers and sometimes Daddy.

◆ ◆ ◆

What do you like to do best?

Collect pets and boyfriends.

How many do you have?

Five.

Pets?

No. Boyfriends.

How do you get so many?

Oh, their families just move into the neighborhood and I grab them.

◆ ◆ ◆

I have a dog.

What kind is it?

Half cocker spaniel and half my neighbor's.

One day the teacher tipped me off that a little boy had been bragging about his pet turtle named "Napoleon." I thought this might be good for some banter, so I brought up the subject:

Got a pet?
    I've got a dog.
Is that all?
    Yep.
Didn't you ever have anything else? Like a turtle?
    Oh. Once we had a turtle. But my brother
flushed *him* down the toilet.

◆ ◆ ◆

    Then there was the boy who announced,
"I have a dog named Petey who can do all
kinds of tricks."
What tricks have you taught him?
    He can sit up, shake hands, and roll over
. . . but the best trick is that he can go to the
bathroom outside.

◆ ◆ ◆

Do you have any pets? I asked another youngster.
Have you ever taught them any tricks?
    Yes.
What?
    I taught the rooster to chase the hens.

Chapter 10

Brethren and Sistern

I WAS an only child. I missed the fun and fights, the laughter and tears of a big family. "Only" children get too much attention part of the time and not enough the rest. The fierce loyalties and the jealous arguments so common in families of six or seven were unknown to me until I raised my own five. I see now how much there is that an only child loses. And perhaps that is why I so often talk to my young guests about this subject. Their answers should educate others like me, and amuse those of you who lived through the scraps between brothers and sisters—the survival of the fittest in the family jungle.

The excitement attendant on the arrival of a new member of the family is a prime topic that elicits some very astonishing answers. One youngster told me that "My mother's sick and tired of waiting for the baby to get here."

"When is it actually expected?"

"Any time now. Mother's been waiting for almost a month."

Then there was the rather confused young man who was only four years old himself.

"We have a new baby about a week old."

"Is it a boy or a girl?"

"So far, I think it's a boy."

"So far," I echoed, "what does it look like?"

"A girl."

An equally equivocal statement came from the girl who admitted she would very much like to have a baby in the family, but: "Mother says we can't have one because Daddy's away digging in the hills somewhere."

THE EASY KIDDING of the "baby" subject that occurs in large families is something the uninitiated can never fully appreciate. What must appear as either "shocking" or "indecent" to a spinster is only the intimate familiarity that exists any place where youngsters are appearing with considerable regularity. Here's an example:

"The teacher tells me something exciting is about to happen at your house."

"Oh, you mean about the boxer dog?"

"No. I understand it's about your mother."

"Oh, that's nothing. She's just going to have another baby."

"That sounds exciting to *me*. Do you want a sister?"

"It had better be a sister."

"What do you mean *better be*?" I was surprised at the belligerent tone.

"My daddy says if it's a boy he's going to drown himself."

I waited for a moment of shocked silence from the audience. Then, choosing my words carefully, I said, "Do you believe him, now, *really*?"

"No. He says this every time and then laughs. He says he might be drowning the wrong man."

ANOTHER LITTLE "rascal" had ears big enough to catch this bit of by-play:

"We have five kids in the family. But there's never going to be another one."

"How can you be sure?"

"Because Daddy says every sixth baby in the world is Chinese, and we don't want one."

MOTHER'S LITTLE helpers learn early in the game some of the hazards involved in bringing up a family. And here's a vivid word picture of one of them:

"We have a five-month-old baby in our family."

"I hope you help your mother . . ." I encouraged her to go on.

"Oh, I wash the baby, change her pants, rock her to sleep, vacuum, make the beds, wash her clothes, and feed the pabulum."

"Then, what does your mother do?"

"She plays gin rummy." (Mother, out in the audience, gave an audible shriek.)

"Which is the worst job of the lot?" I disregarded the shocked interruption.

"Feeding pabulum."

"Why?"

"She sneezes."

A baby's sneeze at precisely the wrong time has redecorated many a nursery, and this answer brought back some of those dark moments to me with a snap. Another disaster type event in family history was recalled by the boy who said:

"My job is to put on the diapers. There are only three main troubles. The old ones stink. The new ones fall off. And the damned baby wiggles."

THE CHILDREN who have no brothers or sisters are fairly agile in inventing them, and their expectations have every assurance of reality—at first. Listen:

"My dad's a cop, but he's learning to do something else."

"What's that?"

"Have a baby."

"That's rather surprising. What does your mother say?"

"Oh, she's the one who gave him the idea. She said if there was going to be another baby in the family, *he'd* have to have it."

"What does your dad say about *that*?"

"He says it'll take at least five years."

I'd like to hear the conversation down at the police station when news of the officer's astounding new aspiration gets around the precinct. Here's another science-fiction story I enjoyed:

"The teacher tells me that you've been talking about someone at your house having a baby. Do you want to tell us about it?"

"It's *me*!"

"*You're* going to have a *baby*? How old are you?" I kidded.

"Almost six."

"When are you going to have this baby?"

"Probably next year."

"Why wait so long?" I teased.

"Gee, I've got to get a *husband* first."

Typical of an only child is the wish of a little girl for a baby sister. She said:

"If I had a magic ring I'd turn it round three times and wish for a sister."

"Yes, but you *don't* have a magic ring, do you?" I objected, to see her reaction.

"I'm going to talk my mother into having one," she answered wistfully.

"How soon?"

"Oh, almost anytime. Some day when she's not doing anything else."

After the broadcast, a pretty little woman looked me up backstage and identified herself as the mother of the girl. "You're going to be a godfather by this time next year," she said. "When my little girl talks like that, I'm going to *find* a day when I haven't anything else to do!"

AND HERE ARE some more penetrating glimpses into life among the siblings:

You say you have a brother . . . what sort is he?

He's a sort of an impossible human being.

How old are you?

Six.

You have about a half dozen teeth out; how did that happen?

This one fell out, this one by pliers, this one by a rock, and this one my sister knocked out with a hammer.

◆ ◆ ◆

Have any brothers or sisters?
Three sisters who live in Portland.
What are they doing up there?
Two of them have babies.
Well, then, do you know what that makes you?
No.
You're an uncle!
Oh no, I'm not. I won't *live* in Portland.

◆ ◆ ◆

What would you do if I gave you five dollars to spend this afternoon?
First, I'd buy my little brother some toys and then I'd buy myself a game.
That's very sweet of you to think of your little brother—and first, too.
Oh, I *have* to buy him something first. If I don't he just messes around with the things I buy for myself.

◆ ◆ ◆

You have wonderful looking teeth. How do you keep them that way?
I sneak into my big brother's bathroom and use his big red toothbrush when he's not looking.

◆ ◆ ◆

What can't you do around the house that you would like to do?
Beat up my sister.

What don't they let her do that she would like to do?

Beat me up.

Why don't you like each other?

We do, but the most fun is beating each other up.

◆ ◆ ◆

How big a family have you?

Four brothers and three sisters.

How do you like that?

It's swell. Everybody has somebody else they can boss.

◆ ◆ ◆

Any brothers?

Two.

What ages?

Fourteen and fifteen.

What type of fellows are they?

Fighting Irishmen.

Real Irish, eh?

Well, half Irish and half brat.

◆ ◆ ◆

Any brothers or sisters?
  No.
What would you like?
  A Pekingese.

◆ ◆ ◆

Do you have any brothers or sisters?
  No.
Which would you like?
  It depends on how much money we have.
What do you mean?
  Well, brothers cost about three million dollars apiece.
They do? Well, what about sisters?
  About a million, one of those would cost.
What would you say a cocker spaniel costs?
  About two million.

◆ ◆ ◆

Any brothers or sisters?
  Yes, a five year old sister.
Does she ever annoy you?
  I'll say! She always wakes me up in the middle of the night to scratch her back.
You might just as well be married.

◆　◆　◆

Any brothers or sisters?
　No.
How do you feel about being an only child?
　I like it; if I had a brother it would just cut into my allowance.

◆　◆　◆

Have you any married sisters?
　One's married, and one has a broken leg.

◆　◆　◆

Do you have any brothers or sisters?
　I have a brother.
How old?
　Three months.
What is he doing these days?
　Mostly riding his bike.

◆　◆　◆

Any brothers or sisters?
　A six year old sister.
What does she do most of the time?
　Picks fleas off our cat.
What kind of cat?
　Well, we had it in the male cage but it turned out to be a female.
How did you find out?
　He had three babies and he's going to have some more.
Who told you?

Nobody, but I can feel them kicking and scratching inside her tummy.

◆ ◆ ◆

Do you have any brothers or sisters?
   No, I'm single.

◆ ◆ ◆

Are you an only child?
   No, I have a brother.
What's his age?
   I don't know his *age* but he's four years old.

◆ ◆ ◆

Any brothers or sisters?
   A sister.
How old?
   Month old.
What does she do most of the time?
   Plays on the back fence.
How can she do that?
   She's a cat.

◆ ◆ ◆

Do you have any brothers or sisters?
   Five brothers.
How old are they?
   The youngest is seventeen and the oldest is thirty-nine.
How old is your mother?
   Forty-one.

◆ ◆ ◆

Any brothers or sisters?

A brother, but what I want most is a sister.

Why do you need a sister?

Because we play Roy Rogers and Dale Evans and we can't really play it until we get a Dale Evans.

◆ ◆ ◆

How many brothers and sisters do you have?

Four brothers and one sister.

What's the biggest problem in growing up in a large family?

The fight to see who gets first in line to take a bath. The last one has to use cold water.

Do you like hot water baths?

I don't know; I've never had any.

◆ ◆ ◆

What does your brother do?

He's in the airborne division in North Carolina.

Does he write home about any exciting experiences?

Oh, yes. He sprained his ankle and broke his leg and the last time he jumped he had to be pushed.

What's your worst bad habit?

My brother; I've had him six and a half years now.

Any brothers or sisters?

No.

What would you like to have?

A sister.

Why?

Because she could make the beds, do the dishes and run errands for me.

You don't want a sister–you want a slave!

That's right.

Do you have any brothers or sisters?

No, I'm an only child.

Do you wish for one?

Yes, I wish we had a sister and my mother wishes we had a brother.

What does your dad wish?

He says he doesn't want any part in it at all.

♦ ♦ ♦

Any brothers or sisters?
One brother.
How many would you like to have?
Three sisters and three brothers.
What do your mother and dad say when you tell them that?
Nothing. They just sit and laugh and laugh.

◆ ◆ ◆

Do you have any brothers or sisters?
No.
Oh, you're a lonesome girl . . . huh? Would you like to have some?
Yes.
Have you spoken to your mother and father about it?
Yes.
What did they say?
No.
Why did they say no?
I guess they're too old.
Well that could happen. How old is your father do you think?
I think twenty-eight.
How old would you guess your mother is?
Sixty-eight.
Sixty-eight. Miss Hanford, my suggestion to you, and this is purely on a friendly basis, you understand. . . . My suggestion is that you never return home.

◆ ◆ ◆

Any brothers or sisters?

A brother two months old.

Do you like him?

Sure. I wanted him even though my daddy didn't.

What do you mean?

Daddy and I had a big argument last year, he said he didn't want him and I said I did.

Then what happened?

Well, one arrived this year, so I guess Daddy knows who's boss.

TAKE THE SUBJECT of brand new brothers and sisters. Five year olds have very definite plans about this even if their parents don't.

"The teacher tells me that on the way down here today you were telling the other kids that something exciting is going to happen around your house pretty soon . . . you're expecting something, aren't you? Tell us about it."

"I'm expecting a baby."

"Well, isn't there somebody else involved besides you?"

"My mother is."

"Well, that's good. I'm glad that you're giving *her* a little bow!"

"And the angels are going to bring it."

"And the angels are going to bring the baby . . . well, how soon are you expecting it?"

"Two weeks."

"In two weeks! Gee, that's exciting. Do you have any brothers and sisters?"

"Yeah, one boy and his name's David."

"How old is he?"

"Two months."

"Well, all I've got to say is the angels have speeded up their delivery this year — they're on a new schedule."

I WONDER HOW many good resolutions are made as a result of my talks with youngsters. As every parent knows, a child will tell a friendly stranger things he wouldn't breathe at home. And wise parents keep their ears open when their youngsters are confiding in non-family friends. I asked one boy if the new year had brought any resolutions to his family circle.

"Yeah, but they're no good."

"What do you mean?"

"My dad got fat last year and made a resolution to get up every morning at six and run around the block."

"What happened?"

"He hasn't been up before nine all year!"

I asked one boy if he could guess why his mother fell in love with his dad.

"Because he knows so many funny stories," came back the answer promptly.

"Why not tell us some?"

"I don't know any good jokes. The only ones I ever hear are the ones my dad tells."

I QUERIED A cute little redhead one day: "Who do you look like in your family?"

"Like my mother," she giggled. "We have

the same color eyes, ears, and hair. And we both have a mole in the same place but I promised I wouldn't say *where*."

Another redhead tossed her head of flaming red curls at my question about "looks" and tartly said: "I don't look like anyone in the family."

"Then, where did you get your red hair?" I ran my fingers through a long curl.

"My mother says 'The Milkman,'" she exploded with laughter. And so did everyone else. Except maybe Dear Old Dad.

Speaking of milkmen, there was a precocious boy visiting us one day who claimed that his mother called him "Farmer John." When I asked him further about this nickname, he said:

"I like farms, and my specialty is raising calves and milking cows."

"I'll bet you don't even know where milk comes from," I teased.

"I sure do. I'm a professional milking kid."

"All right." I was hooked and I knew it. "How do you do it?"

"You grab those faucets hanging down there, fasten the machine on and let 'er rip!"

When you ask a six year old about the secrets of nature you take your career over its highest hurdles. Too many members of the younger generation know too much for their own good and too little for the sake of accuracy. One young fellow confided that if he could be an animal, he'd like to be a horse.

"What kind of a horse?" said I, thinking of

race horses, work horses and so on.

"A stallion!" he roared. "They're the ones who have all the fun."

A shy five year old confessed that he had sneaked out to the barn on his uncle's farm and tried to milk a cow. It had been quite a brave venture, and I inquired for further details.

"Well," he winced at the memory, "I grabbed hold of one of those things and pulled. And all of a sudden it wee-weed right down my pants."

The Farm Belt must have let out five notches that day from the belly laugh that shook the transmitters from coast to coast.

Chapter 11

Kids:
They're Wonderful

THERE'S nothing that makes a grown-up glow with more comfortable self-righteousness than looking back upon his childhood and remembering how perfect it was . . . in spite of everything. How different it was to the younger generation of today with its mass hysteria and sensationalism.

Kids today are just as human as ever. They have a different set of heroes and villains. They speak as unintelligible a language as kids ever did. They get into as much trouble, and cause their parents as much worry as ever. They'll never change. At least, I pray they never will.

This is not to say that I worship all children. Brats who grab food out of your plate, run over your feet with tricycles, upset ice cream cones in your lap, and butt rudely into your conversation are as welcome as the plague. I'm perhaps even less friendly with these spoiled monsters because I know how unnecessary their behavior is. I refer here to the child who has been raised more or less "ad-lib," without benefit of the hard word "No"—mostly by doting parents who pamper their darling as a genius whose development and free expression should never be restricted. These are the show-offs who whine and argue when their slightest whim is not gratified on the spot. "If Sally can stay up until ten o'clock I'm not going to bed now!" or "If I don't get more pie I'm going to scream!"

The life of a happy home can revolve around a child without spoiling the child—if he knows exactly what he can do and can not do. When he knows that he must be polite, respectful of elders and cheerfully obedient without tantrums then *he's* happier, and so are his parents. So long as it is a battle to find out how much more he can get away with, a child is actually a miserable little animal. Real authority, with well defined limits, gives him peace of mind and security.

Occasionally, a spanking has been known to do wonders. It must be administered judiciously and "on the spot," so that the lesson it is intended to teach has real meaning. There's a story that perfectly illustrates this theory.

A young man had been told about George Washington and the cherry tree. His father had impressed him with the importance of truth at all times. And so, when the outhouse was pushed over on Halloween night, the young son was called on the carpet the following morning by his irate parent.

"Yes, Dad," confessed the boy forthrightly, "I cannot tell a lie. My gang pushed over the outhouse last night."

Promptly the dad upended Junior and gave him a walloping that produced a flood of tears and angry squeals. When the yelps became coherent, it was plain that the boy had quite an argument in his favor: "When George Washington told his dad that *he* cut down the cherry tree, he didn't get a spanking because he told the truth!"

The father reflected for a moment solemnly, and then replied: "Well, son. It's different here. You see, George Washington's father was not *up* in the cherry tree!"

ONE OF THE most appealing remarks I've heard come out of a child was spoken by a four year old who was expressing the dearest wish of her heart:

"I'd like to be king of the United States and have two special maids: The Easter Bunny and Santa Claus."

I wonder what a young fellow's dad said to him recently when he told the absolute truth at one of my broadcasts. I asked him what his Dad did for a living, and he replied blithely: "He has a funny kind of a job downtown at a big hotel."

"What do you mean 'funny kind of a job'?" I asked.

"Well, he's in charge of horse-racing. I think they call him a bookkeeper."

And then there was the little spy who reported that her mother spent hours before the mirror each day putting on makeup. "Why do you suppose ladies do that?" I inquired.

"To cover up the dirty spots!"

GIRLS HATE TO be called tomboys. One guest protested she didn't even like to be near a tomboy. When I asked her what kind of a girl she was and what she liked best, she calmly remarked: "I like to climb trees, slide down poles, walk fences, and have rock fights with my brothers." But she didn't like tomboys!

A seven year old girl showed remarkable judgment in the discussion of secretaries.

"What do you think a boss would like to have most: A pretty one or a smart one?"

"It depends on whether the boss is married."

"What do you mean?" I parried.

"Well, if he's married he'd better pick a smart one."

"What if you were married. What kind of a secretary would you pick for your husband?"

"Well, first of all, she'd be at least forty-five years old. She'd be a brunette and wear glasses, high collars, no lipstick, she'd wear black cotton stockings and be fat."

I hope she doesn't marry the kind of a boy my next young guest might turn out to be:

"I'd like Marilyn Monroe for my mother and Elvis Presley for my dad," he wished.

"That's quite a combination. What's your reasons?"

"Well, I like malted milks and Elvis could mix two at a time by strapping them to his hips while he's singing. And Marilyn Monroe would be a swell mother because when she kissed me goodnight. . . . Wow!"

ON THE SUBJECT of glamour girls, one young fellow wished that if Jayne Mansfield could be his mother, then he'd like me to be his father. When I asked why he was so thoughtful in my behalf, he explained: "I figure you're so friendly with children, I'm sure you could be friendly with her, too." And you know . . . he's *right*!

Whenever I think about wonderful kids, I remember the wonderful one-word answer to one of my questions that may reflect the insecurity of a world where the kids hear about atom bombs, hydrogen bombs, and intercontinental guided missiles. I asked the little boy what he wanted to be when he grew up. He thought a long moment and then said:

"Alive."

The bluest of blue eyes were staring at me as I approached a little girl in a party dress. "What a beautiful young lady we have here," I began.

"And look at those eyes! Anybody else in the family have blue eyes?"

"My dad, my mother, my brother, and my neighbor's cat."

"What does your daddy do?"

"He's a senior accountant and takes care of other people's money."

"And who takes care of *his* money?"

"My mother, of course."

And speaking of daddies and money, there was an explosion heard in the insurance business recently when a young fellow gave us the inside of that vocation:

"My daddy has some kind of a job at an insurance company. That's a place where if a person is thrown out of a window or run over by a car or burned up in a house my daddy reads about it in the paper, and then telephones them to sign a paper so he can pay them a lot of money."

If you think *that's* letting the cat out of the bag, how about this revelation:

"My daddy's in the Army, but it's a big secret and I'm not supposed to tell you, and besides I can't pronounce it."

"You're the only one he's told?" I prodded.

"Oh, no, he's told everybody in the family, and a couple of my uncles, too."

By this time, I should imagine that the "top secret" daddy is sweeping up in a government office in charge of janitor supplies.

SOME BOYS just naturally get into trouble, whether it's talking or acting. Here's a frank confession from a small Huck Finn:

"What kind of a boy am I? Well, I guess kind of troublesome."

"Would you explain that, please?"

"Like if I go into a haunted house, then that's the time the cops are there. Or everytime I throw a rock, it seems to hit a window."

"What are you going to do about it?"

"Shucks, there's nothing I *can* do about it."

Maybe he should get a generous supply of a product wished for by another boy:

"I'd like to have a ton of vanishing cream."

"What in the world for?"

"When I see my big brother go get his boxing gloves to poke me in the nose, I'd put on the cream and just disappear!"

IF YOU NEED further convincing that "Kids Are Wonderful," run your eyes over this selection of random comments picked from the brains of everyday boys and girls, just like those who may be living next door to you—or right in your own home:

"I notice you have a tooth out. How do you think the new tooth knows when to start in?"

"It was the last one out so it ought to be the first one in."

What do you do in the afternoon when you come home from school?

I have to take a rest.

That's good, isn't it?

Oh, yes. I lie down on the couch and pretend I'm surrounded by Indians that are on the warpath and want to scalp me and kidnap my sister.

Do you get much rest that way?

No, but I have a lot of fun.

◆   ◆   ◆

What do you like to do best?

Catch jackrabbits.

How do you do it?

I just stand still like a statue and when a rabbit walks by I grab him by the ears.

Catch many?

Just one so far.

Where is he now?

Under the house having babies.

◆   ◆   ◆

Where does the water in all the big oceans come from?

Water that goes down the drain from my bathtub.

◆   ◆   ◆

The main thing I like to do is after school, I de-flea cats.

◆ ◆ ◆

What's the funniest thing you ever saw?
My mother's nightgown. She has a man's face sort of painted all over the front. And when she walks around the bedroom, the eyes roll around and watch me.

◆ ◆ ◆

What animal would you like to be?
A gorilla.
You really mean it? A big ugly gorilla? A sweet little girl like you!
Oh, I'd love to climb trees and eat bananas.

◆ ◆ ◆

If you were stranded on a desert island, what five things would you take with you?—

◆ Eva Gabor, a speedboat, a grass hut, some apples, and a jug of martinis. (Ten year old boy.)

◆ An air conditioner, lipstick, Alan Ladd, a
bathing suit, and a Bible. (Ten year old girl.)

◆   ◆   ◆

What's the prettiest thing you ever saw?
   Texas.
Why?
   It's so full of scenery.

◆   ◆   ◆

*What's the worst punishment you can think of for a six
year old boy?*
   Well, being hung up on a rope and having
your bare back lashed with a razor strap.
Has this ever happened you? (Incredulously.)
   No. It's just the worst thing I can *think* of.

◆   ◆   ◆

   I'd like to change your program and move it
to another network.
Why do that?
   Because every time I tune in, there's an Indian dancing on your head.

◆   ◆   ◆

   I want to be a shot doctor.
What's that?
   If you have a cold, I'd give you a cold shot.
What if I had measles?
   I'd give you a measles shot.
How about a broken leg?
   I'd give you a broken leg shot.
You're a shot doctor, all right.

◆　◆　◆

Santa Claus has twelve reindeers, but he only uses about ten in the air.
Only ten? What happens to the others?
They're spares.

◆　◆　◆

Where did you get that scratched nose? Have an accident?
It was nothing much. I fell out of the Christmas tree.

◆　◆　◆

What has the dentist done to your teeth?
He pulled one out because it had a pimple on it.

◆　◆　◆

I'm the bravest boy in our block.
How do you know?
I can kill bees with my bare fingers.
My, that is brave. How do you do it?
I sneak up behind them when they're on a flower and squeeze them.
With that kind of nerve, what do you think you'll finally be when you grow up?
A bartender.

◆　◆　◆

Do you have any real problems in life?
When I go to a school dance somebody else always gets the pretty girls, and I'm left with the dregs.

◆ ◆ ◆

See, Mr. Linkletter, I'm wearing suspenders
to hold up my pants. The belt is just for looks.

◆ ◆ ◆

What do you like for breakfast?
   Eggs.
How do you like them?
   With the yellow in them.

◆ ◆ ◆

You're a cub scout aren't you?
   Yes. Our motto is "Be Prepared."
What would you do if you were lost in a forest?
   The thing to do is make a signal fire.
How do you do that?
   You get tinder and flint and rocks and wood.
Have you ever actually tried this?
   Certainly. I've been away out in the moun-
tains.
*My what a good scout you are. After you got every-
thing together, what happened?*
   Nothing.

◆ ◆ ◆

What's the greatest invention of all time?
   The egg beater.
Why?
   Because it's the best thing to lick.

◆ ◆ ◆

Is this your favorite dress?
   No, it's an old one.
Then why did you wear it?
   Because my mother didn't want me to wear any of my nice new dresses to your old program and get them dirty.

◆ ◆ ◆

   I'm from Texas, the most wonderful place in the world.
What do you miss most about it?
   The snakes and the sandstorms.

◆ ◆ ◆

Who's the prettiest woman in the world in your opinion?
   My teacher. Right out there in the audience.
Well, that takes care of your grades for this year. But what about your mother?
   Oh, she's okay I guess, except she runs around the house in her nightgown all day.

◆ ◆ ◆

Say, haven't you a little sniffle this morning?
   Yes, and I have a big sneeze, too.

◆ ◆ ◆

I like to eat turkey the best thing of all.
What part of the turkey?
The part with the meat on it.

◆ ◆ ◆

I've got a new boyfriend (bragged the pretty little girl).
How do you know he's really your boyfriend?
I know because yesterday he told me to shut up and go home.

◆ ◆ ◆

What do you do the last thing before you go to sleep?
Kiss my mommy and daddy and check my money box.

◆ ◆ ◆

I have one little sister named Judy. And we have a baby in escrow.
In escrow? Who told you that?
All I know is that my daddy said so.
What is escrow? Do you have any idea?
Well, my daddy says anything that's in escrow, it seems like it's never going to come out.

◆ ◆ ◆

My sister just had a baby but they didn't tell me whether it's a boy or girl, so I don't know whether I'm an aunt or an uncle.

◆ ◆ ◆

Is your mother with you today?
   Yes, she's the lady in the front row there with the run in her stocking.

◆ ◆ ◆

How are you children all doing in school this year?

◆ I'm first in English.

◆ I'm first in history.

◆ I'm first in the street when the bell rings.

◆ ◆ ◆

I hear you just got over the chicken pox. How was it?
   Nothing to it. All you do is sit in bed and scratch.

◆ ◆ ◆

You should always eat a good breakfast so you'll grow up quicker.
   Not for me. If I grow up faster, I'll get older sooner and then I'll have to die younger.

◆ ◆ ◆

Who's the smartest man in the world?

◆ Abraham Lincoln.
Why?
   Because he fought so well we won the First World War.
Who told you that?
   Nobody. I just know it.

◆ Gene Autry.
Why?
   Because no matter who ties him up he can always get out of it.

◆ God.
Why?
   Because when people are naughty he can take the naughty right out of them.

◆   ◆   ◆

What's your favorite slang expression?
   "Bury that crazy prehistoric!"
What does it mean?
   It means get rid of that old man.
Who do you use it on?
   Anyone over 21.

◆   ◆   ◆

Have any hobbies?
   I like to eat and play the piano—at the same time.
That's quite a trick. How do you do it?
   I play scales with my left hand and eat with my right.

◆   ◆   ◆

What do you want to be?
   An FBI man.
Why?
   Because they're always getting into trouble.

◆   ◆   ◆

What's a bachelor?

He's a guy who has more money than a married man.

Why are taxes necessary?

Well, if you don't have a car you can always call one.

Have you written Santa Claus?

I'd better whisper in your ear or I'm going to spoil Christmas for these other kids.

Do you have a hobby?

I try to get my weekly allowance without doing any work.

If the Good Fairy gave you one wish, what would it be?

I'd like a chemical set.

What would you do with it?

I'd take it way out in the field so if it blew up I'd be the only one to go.

How would you like to surprise your folks?

I'd like to take them home a million dollars.

Where would you get it?

I'd save it out of my allowance.
How much do you get?
Ten cents a week.

◆ ◆ ◆

How old are you?
Five.
Have any idea what you'll be?
School teacher.
Why?
Because you get a dollar a month.
How would you spend that much?
I would save it to buy a couch.
Why would you want a couch?
For my poor husband to lie down on and rest
when he comes home from work.

◆ ◆ ◆

What do you want to be?
A sweeper.
What's that?
Another name for a wife.

◆ ◆ ◆

Any pets?
Some goldfish. They're named Eeny,
Meeny, Miny, and Mo.
How are they?
Dead.
What happened?
They went crazy, then they jumped out of
the bowl and drowned themselves in the air.

◆ ◆ ◆

Do any of you kids have anything important to tell me today?

Well, we saw a dead cat on the way to the studio.

◆ ◆ ◆

What do you want to be?

A singer in church on Sundays and the rest of the week I'll sell candy.

Why did you decide on this?

Because I love to sing "Jesus Loves Me" and eat candy.

◆ ◆ ◆

What bothers you the most?

The long automobile commercials on TV in the middle of English movies because they're hard enough to follow anyway.

◆ ◆ ◆

What's your favorite day of the week?
    Saturday.
Why?
    Because I can stay in bed all morning and coast.
What do you mean "coast"?
    Well, you know. You're not asleep, and you're not awake . . . you're just coasting.

◆ ◆ ◆

I see you have a sore mouth. What happened?
    I ran into a hot marshmallow.
A hot marshmallow?
    Yes, I was eating on one part and didn't notice the other part was on fire.

◆ ◆ ◆

What are you going to be?
    A rocket engineer like my dad.
Where will you go?
    To Mars.
What do you suppose the people on Mars are like?
    Well, their eyes and mouth and nose is down where their belly is and their belly button is up on their forehead.

◆ ◆ ◆

Why were you picked to come on the show?
    Because my teacher says I have a vivid imagination.
What do you want to do when you grow up?
    Be a secretary.

Then what?

Get married.

What do you think makes a good husband?

Someone who brings home presents all the time and doesn't drink.

You know you're lunching with us today. What will you order?

Filet mignon and champagne.

Champagne! And you're going to marry a man who doesn't drink? That does take a vivid imagination!

Well, I'm not married *yet*.

◆　◆　◆

How were you picked for the program?

The teacher gave us all a test in our imagination.

What did you do?

It was easy. I pretended I was an onion.

◆　◆　◆

I heard you had an interesting dream last night. What was it?

I dreamed I was sitting on an incubator and I kept hatching eggs.

◆　◆　◆

Do you have any hobbies?

Yes, I collect diamonds.

Where do you get them?

On the floor at Sears Roebuck.

◆　◆　◆

What would you like to invent?

A way for people to be invisible.
Why?
Because when my mother gets mad I like to disappear.

◆   ◆   ◆

What would you like to invent?
Some Zippo shoes. When you press a button they walk you, or dance you, or run you.

◆   ◆   ◆

What secret do you have from your folks?
I'm keeping a rat under my bed.
Where did you get it?
I caught it when it ran across the floor.
What else have you got there?
A horse.
What's it doing under there?
Just sleeping.
You're just making all this up, aren't you?
Yes.

◆   ◆   ◆

What did you dream last night?
That a big elephant swallowed me.

How terrible! What then?
   It was all right. He burped, and I jumped out
and ran home.

◆ ◆ ◆

How would you change the world?

◆ I'd have hospitals for well people so they
could go and have orange juice and breakfast
in bed and pretty nurses and have a good time
when they could enjoy it.

◆ I'd invent a dishwasher that had a lot of arms
on it so it could scrape and clean the dishes first,
then wash and dry them and put them away.

◆ I'd invent a rocket so I could leave the world.
Then I wouldn't have to worry about inventions.

◆ ◆ ◆

What's a road hog?
   It's a big animal you see on the road and if
you catch it you take him home and eat him.

◆ ◆ ◆

Any hobbies?
   I collect mice.
Where do you get them?
   I catch them around the house.
How many do you have now?
   None; they all died.
What will you do for a hobby now?
   I think mountain climbing.

◆ ◆ ◆

What will you be when you grow up?
A mother with ten kids, a million dogs and a million cats and one rabbit.

◆ ◆ ◆

What do you like to do best?
Fly kites. I have a secret invention, where instead of using one long tail, I use a third string which runs over and connects with the second one that's connected with the tail and it loops over to the first string and one secret one. *Well, don't let anybody know. . . .*

◆ ◆ ◆

How old are you?
Six.
Any hobbies?
I like to drive cars.
When do you ever drive?
I don't yet because of one trouble.
What's that?
My mother won't give me the keys.

◆ ◆ ◆

What do you want to be?
A carpet layer during the week and a preacher on Sunday.
Why?
My dad is a carpet layer and my mother wants me to go to heaven.

◆ ◆ ◆

What's your name?
Alex Fontainbleu.
What kind of name is that?
French.
What's your father?
Part Scotch, part English and Irish.
What's your mother?
Swedish.
What does that make you?
I'm Spanish.

How old are you?
Four.
What do you want to be?
I don't want to be anything.
Don't you want to get married?
Yes.
How'll you get the money?
My wife can work.
What if she won't?
I'll send for my mother.

◆ ◆ ◆

Do you have any hobbies?
Yes, collecting brothers.
How many have you?
Only one, so far, but I'm looking for another one any day now.
Oh, then your mother's expecting?
No, my brother's expecting. He got married last month.

◆ ◆ ◆

What is your idea of the definition of a gentleman?

◆ A man who cleans up after himself in the bathroom.

◆ A man who's always nice to his wife and hardly ever hits her.

◆ A man who always picks up a handkerchief that's dropped except by another man.

◆ A man who always kisses his wife just before he leaves for work.

◆ ◆ ◆

What's your definition of maturity?
   It's when you come to a dead end.

◆ ◆ ◆

Have any hobbies?
   I collect diamonds.
Where do you get them?
   From my oldest sister.
Where does she get them?
   From her boyfriends.

◆ ◆ ◆

What would you like to be?
   A nurse.
Who would you practice on?
   My sister.
How?
   I'd give her shots.
Where?
   Every place.

◆ ◆ ◆

What's new?
   We had a big birthday party yesterday and I won the main prize.
How did you do it?
   I pinned the tail on the donkey and I won. I always win.
What's your method for winning this game?
   I peek through the blindfold.

◆ ◆ ◆

What kind of a haircut is that?
   A flat top.
Do you like it?
   No, I like a butch.
Then why did you get a "flat top"?
   Well, I ordered a butch, but the barber goofed.

◆ ◆ ◆

How would you change school?
   I'd change the seats from hard wood to foam

rubber.
Why?
   I'm not going to say right here . . . but you know!

◆   ◆   ◆

What do you want to be?
   A football player until the season's over, then I'll be a baseball player until I'm old, and then I'll be a doctor so I can get hold of a great big building full of money like my grandfather.

◆   ◆   ◆

What are some of the sayings that ten year olds are using around school these days?

◆ "Go, man, go!"

◆ "He's a cube." (That means dope.)

◆ "She's 3-D." (Dizzy, dopey, and dumb.)

◆ "Jet propelled muscle juice."
What's that?
   Milk.

◆   ◆   ◆

What do you want to be?
   Superman.
What's so attractive about that?
   Well, he flies around and knocks people down.
What are you doing to practice for that kind of job?

I'm a super-boy. I practice knocking my little brother down.

What makes a man bald?
They eat too much . . . It fills them up so much that it pushes the hair right through the top.

Chapter 12

Kids Write *the Darndest Things!*

To MOST KIDS in grammar school, the idea of writing to the King of England, the President of the United States, or God, is no more frightening than leaving a note for the family milkman. They are unfazed by movie stars, astronauts, or even Santa Claus. And when they are encouraged by imaginative teachers to express their thoughts on paper to high ranking personalities, some of the most hilarious epistles in the history of the post office are the result.

In my own case, following a lecture on the subject of drug abuse at the Elementary School of Appleton, Wisconsin, I received several of the most surprising letters of my life. I'm sure the idea of writing me was not their own. Their teachers most probably told them that after they had written to that nice Mr. Linkletter, they could go out to play. Hence, the deluge of block-lettered, smudgy scrawls arrived in Hollywood in due time.

◆ "Dere Mister Inkletter: Thank you fir comming to our schoool and leading us into drug abuse!" That was the sum and substance of one dubiously flattering letter.

◆ "Dear Linklettuce: You are the best talker I have ever herd.
P.S. You are the only talker I have ever herd."
   (Probably the most honest letter I have ever received.)

◆ "Dere Art: I bet you talked good. Everboddy says so. I wasent there. I am sorry. I wet my pants and was in the boys room." (That's reason enough!)

◆ "Hello: How are you? I am fine. Now I can go play ball. Goodbye."

"THE THINGS children say and write, in their own kind of wisdom, help us to reexamine the world." This was said by a President of the United States who permitted me to reprint some of the letters that had been sent to him by the future voters of the country. He went on: "I have benefited from the unique insight of the letters that have come to the White House. There are sense and comedy, sadness and fantasy, delight and profundity in what they have to say."
   Here, then, are some of my favorites:

◆ "Dear President: I wanted to let you know I like you, and I don't care how big your nose is. You can always count on me."

◆ "Dear Mr. President: Our family has two cats, three dogs, a parrot, and I have a can of ten worms. They all depend on us for food and water. So why can't we get a refund on our income taxes?"

◆ "Dear Chief: I think pollution is terrible. You should go on television and tell people how it kills animals, and makes the water dirty. Pretty soon we will all have to wear gas masks. Even my mother is polluting rivers. She uses deterrents."

◆ "Dear President: If you keep on doing so great, I'll bet you will probably go down in history like Rodolf the Red Nose Raindear."

◆ "Dear Sir: I saw you call the moon on T.V. Sunday night. I called the operator and asked to speak to the moon. She said 'When you get the number, I will get you through.' Tell me: Is it an unlisted number?"

◆ "Mr. President: Here is my question. If you were ten years old, how would you help your country?"

◆ "Greetings: I have been thinking about Veet Nam. Wowdn't it be cheaper to buy it?"

AND AMONG the "fun" letters there are poignant cries to help:

"Dear Mr. President: I hope you have the extra time to read my letter. I am writing to let you know the good things and the bad things. A president is something like a father you can go to the president to listen to your problems as well as your father. The teen-agers that are in the streets today it is just outrageous. There are so many bad things I can't describe them all. You know what they are. 'Please!' try to help us."

◆   ◆   ◆

"I am writing to tell you about Detroit. I live in the slums of Detroit. I often walk down the street and just stare at the sidewalks. It hurts me just to look at all of the filth and garbage. I have two sisters and one brother. I don't want the smallest one growing up in a neighborhood like this. I love to go to Bell Isle and watch the fountain at night. It changes colors. I only get to go sometimes. You know how it is. If you understand."

◆   ◆   ◆

◆ "Dear Mr. President: What is your favorite sport? Mine is eating."

◆ "Dear Sir: You probably think I have some nerve to write to the President. Well, maybe you will answer. (I hope) I am age 11, sixth grade, brown hair, blue eyes and 5 feet! That's me, all over. I spended a whole night planning this letter. I would like to become Pen-Pals because I can help you and you can help me with my problems. You can think about it and write. I must go to bed, so fare well."

◆ " Dere Mister: I am a Baptist and a Brownie. Can I join the Republicans besides, or would this give me a conflicting interest?"

◆ "Mister President: I want to be like you and do what you do. What do you do?"

◆ "Dear Mr. President: I am ready to be a national hero. Please send instructions."

◆ "Dear President: I am Cathatic. What nationality are you?"

◆ "Dear President of the U.S.A.: For my class project I am to get all the information about birth control. Can you help me, or am I too expectant?"

◆ "Dear President: According to what I have for my report, our American population is thickening more than a million a year. This means that, play like it is 2000 A.D. there are more than 300 million of us. Is any of this true or false?"

And, finally, my favorite:

◆ "Dere Mister President. I would like you to send children Mars in the next space ship going in that direction. I would appreciate it very much if I could go. One of your future voters: Mitchell." (Attached note: "Dear Mr. President: As the parents of Mitchell Miller, we would like to give you our permission to send Mitchell anywhere into space.")

SUNDAY SCHOOL teachers occasionally ask their young Bible students to write a letter to God, instead of praying out loud. Here are a few of my favorites:

◆ "Dear God: Count me in. Your friend, Herbie."

◆ "Dear God: I read your book. It's great. Keep up the good work. Jackie."

◆ "Dear God: I feel sorry for boys and girls who have no parents. When Jesus was born, he became the father of everyone who has no mother or dad. I hope this is true because I am one."

◆ "Dear God: I want to be a Sunday School teacher when I grow up because you only work one day a week."

◆ "Dear God: I borrowed a cooky last week when my Mom wasn't watching. Were you?"

◆ "Dear God: We're Baptists and I want to make sure I get into heaven. I know that St. Peter is right there at the gate. Is he one, too?"

◆ "Dear God: I have heard that when Jesus returns there will be great happiness. Some will be reunited with loved ones in Heaven. Others with their husbands."

◆ "Dear God: I love the Bible so far. I know about the Creation, the Flood, and the Battle of

Jericho. It's so exciting. I never know what you'll do next."

◆ "Dear God: Are boys better than girls. I know you are one . . . but try to be fair. Sylvia."

AT ONE POINT, on our *House Party* program, I asked viewers to send in samples of the darndest things their kids had written. The result was an epidemic of sprained backs among Los Angeles mail-carriers and a wave of total inefficiency in my office, where people sat around reading and laughing all day instead of doing any work. I can only offer you a tiny sampling of these masterpieces, but here are a few.

Schoolteachers, naturally, had the widest selection of gems from compositions, themes, excuses, and so on. Here's a somewhat puzzled nine year old writing a report on baby chickens:

"A baby chicken leads a very interesting life. It begins when the mother has the egg. It is a very hard sturrogle to come out of the egg. I'm not sure, but I think the Father has something to do with it. By that I mean I think the Father lays eggs too."

She must have been a city youngster. Like the kid I heard of who was visiting his country cousin and spotted some empty milk bottles in the grass. "Come quick, Johnny," he yelled. "I've found a cow's nest!"

One teacher sent me some interesting ideas that she got from her third-graders when she asked for a one-paragraph essay on "How I Would Change History."

"At the beginning," wrote a young lady named Kathy Tyler, "I would make all the people without bones. Then they would be loose. Then we would crawl and things would be slow."

They sure would, Kathy!

In that same class, a young man named Stuart Shapiro had a more practical idea. "If I could change history," he wrote, "I would leave out the part that is taught in school."

Another viewer sent in the following "Little Boy's Essay on Anatomy," which I regard with a certain amount of suspicion because it is almost too good to be true:

"Your head is kind of round and hard and your brains are in it and your hair is on it. Your face is in front of your head where you eat and make faces. Your neck is what keeps your head out of your collar. It's hard to keep clean. Your shoulders are sort of shelfs where you hook suspenders on.

"Your stumick is something that if you do not eat often enough—it hurts, and spinach don't help it none. Your spine is a long bone in your back that keeps you from folding up. Your back is alway behind you no matter how quick you turn around. Your arms have got to pitch with and so's you can reach the butter, and they keep your hands from falling off. Your fingers stick out of your hand so you can throw a curve and add up 'rithmetick. Your legs is what, if you have not got two of, you can't get to first base. Your feet are what you run on, your toes are what always get stubbed. And that's all there is of you except what's inside, and I never saw it."

TEACHERS ARE always getting excuse notes for one thing or another. Here's one from a little boy who lost his "absence" excuse and prepared his own:

"Dear Teacher: Please excuse Buddy for being absent yesterday. He was absent because he didn't go to school."

And here's one handed in instead of the assigned homework:

"Dear Teacher: I tried to do my arithmetic, but I couldn't do some of them and I didn't have time to do the ones I could do."

I also got a chuckle out of this one, addressed to a teacher who had had to leave school because she was pregnant:

"Dear Teacher: We miss you. We are all fine. How are you filling?"

And then there was the kid who was designing a safety poster warning his classmates not to play with old lumber. This was his slogan: It is dangerous to play with old broads!

If you don't think the love-bug bites early and hard nowadays, cast your eye on this bashful communication intercepted by a vigilant third-grade teacher:

"Dear John,

Please exquse the paper please. If you would take me to some secrut place do you know what Id do? If you were coming near a bush where I was hiding Id grab you pull you in—slang expreshun—and *KISS YOU*.

Love, Barbara.

P.S. How about going steady, PLEASE?"

It looks as if the male of the species is getting more elusive than the female. Down in Memphis, Tennessee, when he received an ardent declaration of love from a young lady acquaintance, Allen Carson, age eight, sat down and wrote his admirer a firm note:

"Dear Sally, I don't love you at all. All my love, Allen."

While out in Whittier, California, a young lady summed up her love life to date in the following poignant essay entitled "The Bravest Thing I Ever Did."

"I kissed a boy in fourth grade when he gave me a present and I didn't like him and I still don't."

And here's one from a mother whose stay in the hospital was lightened by a dispatch from the home front:

"Dear Mommie, I am trying to be a good boy While you are gone. I found Grandpa's pipe and smoked it a little. It didint taste good and it made me feel rite loneskome. uncle henry said there was a looney tick loose in the woods I think it aint so. we looked for it and oney found some wood ticks How does a looney tick look? we dont keep the house much clean Daddy said we would clean it up before you came home. I didint know if I should ask the Lord to make you better. He might think I dont trust the doctor. Grandpa said I could pray for the doctor. I wash my ears each day I send you love I wish you was home.

Yours truly, Paul."

Professional writers say you should leave something to the imagination of the reader. Here's an excerpt from the letter of an eight year old who is already a master. She's writing to her older sister who's away at school:

"Mother had a hard time today, she fell down and tore her new stockings, then a mouse ran up her leg. Daddy looked for it and couldn't find it . . ."

Then she added a couple of pages of household news, and, as an afterthought:

"P.S. The mouse ran down again."

Here's a cure for a cold from a young man who obviously can't spell *cathartic*:

"Go home, gargle your throat, take a good Catholic, and go to bed."

I heard a good writer say once that the most effective way to write is just the way you talk, relaxed and natural. Here's an exponent of that school, age eight, writing to the parents of her best friend:

"Dear Mrs. Corton and Mr. Corton, I think Marion is getting to be an ofel bad girl and you will never catch me playing with her again nor talking with her again she said if my house got struck with lightning I could not go over to her house and i said if hers did she could not come over to my house and she said she did not want to come over to my house because it was to dirty and she taught me to say O my god and I am going to pay her back because she has been ofel greedy with me for a long time and i did not want to tell you on the 21 of August she slapped the baby just as hard as she could because he wet his pants and I am just going to give every body presents but marion. good-bye from Jessie."

Kids are wonderfully casual when it comes to that precious commodity, time. Here's a note a friend of mine found on her return from a shopping trip:

"Dear Mother, I have gone fishing. What time shall I come home? Love, Leonard."

Another youngster left this invitation for his grandparents:

"Dear Grandma and Grandpa, Mom wants you to come to dinner tonight if you get home before six. Love, Mike.

P.S. We are eating at four."

DISCIPLINARY action on the part of the parents sometimes results in notes, penitent and otherwise. One six year old, sent to her room for being naughty, was told she couldn't come out until she agreed that she had been a bad girl. Half an hour later a "sirrender nowte" was pushed under the door:

"Dear Dadd, I am a stooput brat I hat myself from Bad Linda."

But sometimes mixed reactions show through. Here's a sample from a smoldering ten year old:

"Daddy. I don't know about liking you. If you keep after me I will hate you for sure. If you will stop getting after me I will love you better than I do now. From your half loving half hating girl to her half loving half hating Daddy."

Sometimes a line in a letter will be more revealing than the kid knows. Here's one from a twelve year old who had just returned to school:

"We got here in a hurry. The man who drove stopped on the road and drank two cans of oil."

Sometimes kids are more grateful for T.L.C. (Tender Loving Care) than we realize. Here's a note from an eight year old in Worcester, Massachusetts:

"Dear Mommy, I am very forchenard to have a mother who would want to get up two times at night to give me medissin. I know that you are very tired and I know that some night God forbid you should be sick I will get up to give you some medissin. I am very forchenard to have you and Daddy as parents. Because if you were not my parents I might still be sick. All I can say is thank you very much. Love, Ann"

While out in Vernal, Utah, the guardians of the law received this communication from a conscience-stricken eight year old:

"Dear Poleece, I do not want to say this but I will. It is very bad news. I am a robber."

Here's an excerpt from an eleven year old's diary that, needless to say, has stuck in my memory:

"Dear Diary: Well, another day is here. It is just like all days. I just sit rond doing nothing but watch TV. I watched Art Linklitter and then I got sick. Well I better go now."

And here are some dreams confided to his diary by a nine year old:

"I would like to be father of two children and president of a bank. Because I like kids and banks. To be president of a bank you have to have a good record and no time in the pen. To be a father it's natural and easy."

LETTERS from camp would fill a book, and a pretty funny book at that. Here are a few samples of unadorned camper's prose:

◆ "Dear Mom and Dad, I'm not a bit homesick. Some of the kids are. The ones who have dogs . . ."

◆ "Dear Mom and Dad, I have a big part in the camp play. It's about the pied piper. I am one of the rats. . . ."

◆ "Dear Mother, I am scribbling this note standing up because last night my bunk burned down. Nothing much happens here."

◆ "Dear Dad, I am having a good time. Can you please send me some city eggs? I don't like country eggs."

◆　◆　◆

Inevitably there are a few wistful souls who wish they were anywhere but in camp, although sometimes they make a valiant effort to conceal it. Here's a brave try:

"Dear Mom and Dad, I am not homesick. Please write to me. Are you coming Sunday. Please come. I need some clean towels. Write and tell me if you are coming. Please come and bring the baby. They keep us so busy here I don't have time to get homesick. Please come Sunday. Love, Paul. P.S. Next year I think I'll come to camp for the shorter period."

◆　◆　◆

Here's a young man who gets the same message across with fewer words: "Dear Mom, there is a hundred and fifty boys in this camp. I wish it was a hundred and forty-nine."

◆　◆　◆

I think the one that tickled me most was this note that the fond parents received from their eleven year old:

"Dear Mother and Daddy, your worries are over. I am really growing up. I'm in a tent with older girls and all we talk about is boys and sex. Please send me a water pistol. Love, Linda"

◆　◆　◆

Here's a solicitous camper, thinking of other people's welfare:

"Dear Mom and Dad: Don't touch this postcard. I have poison ivy. Love . . ."

How's this for social progress? It's a camp letter from a ten year old:

"Dear Mother, The first day here I didn't have *hardly* any friends. The second day I had a *few* friends. The third day I had *friends* and *enemies*. Love, Anna"

Here's a resourceful young fellow:

"Dear Mom, I can't find my St. Christopher medal anywhere but do not worry. I have the St. Joseph's aspirin you put in my bag, so I will probably be okay."

The world can seem like an unfriendly place when you're only eight years old and away from home for the first time. This was Kathy's first communication from camp:

"Dear Mom, The foode is good, the camp is good, the wetter is good, the counseler is good, but—when you come to visit me, pleeze take me home—good. Love, kathy."

Little boys are made of sterner stuff—like this one: "Dere Mom, yesterday on a hike I almost stepped on a snake and that snake was six feet—and boy that's some tall snake!"

◆   ◆   ◆

Here's true filial devotion for you:

"Hello Mom and Pop. They just told us that we cant eat until we write our parnts so I am just going to write enough this time to get something to eat. Love, Bud."

◆   ◆   ◆

So it goes, from the first of July every summer to the end of August. And sometimes even the camp authorities get into the act. Here's a note received by some friends of mine:

"Dear Friends, we are happy to be able to tell you, and we are sure that you will be proud to learn, that your son is now an Advanced Non-Swimmer."

NO COLLECTION of kid letters would be complete without a couple addressed to that lovable old gentleman with the red suit and white beard who lives at the North Pole, so here are a few:

◆ "Dear Santa, I guess I have been half good and half bad most of this year so you can just send me half of what I ask for."

◆ "Dear Santa, is it true that you don't come down chimneys any more? My Daddy says you come through a large hole in his pocketbook."

◆ "Dear Santa, I am 6½ years old. Two years ago I asked for a baby sister and I got it. Last year I asked for a baby brother to play with and I got it. So this year if it's alright with Mommy and Daddy I would like to have a pony."

◆ "Dear Santa, . . . and I want a washcloth for Granny's cat so he won't wear out his tongue."

◆ "Dear Santa, . . . what I'd like most of all, if your reindeer have any babies, would be to have a little baby reindeer for my own."

◆ "Dear Santa, . . . and please could you bring Daddy some of whatever kind of hair tonic is what you use? His head is beginning to come up through his hair."

◆ "Dear Santa, . . . and please bring a bed for my Daddy. I have a little bed, sister has a little bed, Mommy has a bed, and poor Daddy has no bed—he has to sleep with Mommy."

THE CHARM of the things kids write, like the appeal of the things kids say, lies in the combination of honesty and simplicity and un-expectedness. You can't imitate it, and you can't fake it. It comes from only one source: the mouths of babes. One more, and then we'll move on. This one came in a note from a lady in Bristol, Connecticut:
"Dear Art,

When my son had his sixth birthday, he received a new wallet. A couple of days later I found the identification card carefully filled out as follows: Name—Charles   Age—6   Hair—brown   Eyes—2."

OH, IT'S a wonderful world, this secret world of kids. There are times when I wish I were back in it myself. But wishing won't make it so. Anyway, here's a thought I came across the other day that I like. I don't know who said it, but he was a wise man:

"You're only young once . . . but that's enough if you work it right."

Chapter 13

Free for All

EVER since I first began talking with children on the air, listeners have been sending along their own favorite "kid stories." Usually these anecdotes are told as if they'd just happened to the storyteller's own bright daughter, niece or nephew, because people sense instinctively that a story sounds funnier if it "really happened."

However, I've run into the same stories so often that unless the long arm of coincidence is flailing around like a punch-drunk windmill, there is some pretty slick plagiarizing going on by fond relatives!

"Dear Mr. Linkletter," writes a father from Walla Walla, Washington, "Here's one that'll fracture you. My little girl, Gloria, came home from school the other day and said, 'I'm not going back. I can't read. I can't write. And they won't let me talk!' Isn't she a cute one to come up with a crack like that?"

Yes, Dad, she *is* a cute one. And that was a cunning remark. And I'll bet that little Willie Shakespeare's dad liked it when he heard it, too. But I'm glad you reminded me, because I'm writing a book. And so, here is my choice of the best stories that have been sent my way by doting parents, fond uncles and admiring friends. Some of them must have actually happened. Others are older than any of us.

This book is supposed to be made up of comments by the kids on my *House Party* show, and nine-tenths of it is. Still I have to be honest enough to admit that, every once in a while, purely by chance, a youngster *not* on my program makes a funny remark. So why hold out on you? Here's your free dividend of more quips, slips, and shockers, straight out of the mouths of babes.

OF ALL THE STORIES I have told at dinners and broadcast warm-ups, this first one has easily won the award for top laughs. Its hero is a tiny Sunday School pupil who had listened wide-eyed to the teacher talking about a Bible lesson that included the quotation about "from dust thou art and to dust thou shalt return." Rushing home from the meeting, he peeked under his bed and then went running to his mother.

"Mama, is it true we're dust before we're born?"

"Well, yes," Mother said. "I believe that's true."

"And Mama, is it true we're dust after we're dead?"

"Of course," Mother replied in a puzzled tone. "Why?"

"Well come up and look under my bed, quick! Somebody's either coming or going!"

◆ ◆ ◆

A little boy was standing on the sidewalk watching the milkman's horse intently. When the driver finally returned from his errands, the youngster inquired, "Do you have much farther to go today?"

"Why, son?" asked the milkman.

"Well, you ain't goin' far," the boy announced. "Your horse just lost all its gasoline."

◆ ◆ ◆

My favorite definition of a child: An object half way between an adult and a television set.

◆ ◆ ◆

A perfect definition of erosion: A nine year old boy washing his hands.

◆ ◆ ◆

A Sunday School teacher was showing her class a picture of the Christian martyrs in a den of lions. One little girl looked so sad as she studied the picture. Finally she exclaimed: "Gee, look at that poor lion 'way in the back. He ain't going to get any."

And did you hear about the skeptical little girl who said: "If George Washington was such an honest man, why do they close all the banks on his birthday?"

A six year old girl received a wrist watch and a bottle of perfume for her birthday. All day long she kept showing everyone her presents, until finally her mother said: "Honey, I know that you're proud of your gifts, but you're bothering everybody with them. You may sit at the dinner table with our guests tonight only if you promise not to mention the watch or the perfume even once."

The little one promised. And all through the dinner she sat wordless, but from time to time sniffing audibly, and at frequent intervals raising her left wrist to her ear to catch the sound of the ticking. Nobody paid her a bit of attention. Finally, in desperation, as the meal came to an end, she blurted out: "I'm not supposed to mention it. But if anybody hears anything or smells anything, it's *me*!"

I have some favorite stories that I tell about my own five little Links. Which ones are strictly authentic, and which ones I have improved upon—well, I'll leave that for you to guess.

When our teen-age Dawn was going to her first serious party and wanted an off-the-shoulder gown to impress everyone, the family had a council meeting to argue the merits and disadvantages of such a "daring" costume. Some argued one way and some argued the other. Finally the sophisticated eighteen year old boy Jack settled the question with one remark: "Put it on her. If it stays *up*, she's old enough!"

Then I tell of young Robert's triumphant return from first grade shouting:

"I can write! I can write!"

In surprise and disbelief, his mother said: "What did you write?"

"How should I know?" he shrugged off the question. "I can't *read*!"

◆ ◆ ◆

And here's a commentary on parents delivered by my youngest youngster while talking of a forthcoming school play: "We're going to have *real* people in the audience—not just mothers and fathers."

The same Link in my family chain loves dogs, so when he saw a magnificent St. Bernard on the leash, he rushed up, hugged him and then began to stroke his long, bushy tail. Moments later, his mother came along and was horrified to see her child clutching the tail of the tremendous animal.

"Get away from that beast!" she shouted. "He'll bite you!"

"Oh, no, Mommy," he reassured her. "This end never bites!"

Definition of adolescence: That period when a boy refuses to believe that someday he'll be as dumb as his father.

Little Susan was inclined to exaggeration. Her stories always seemed so full of adventures, and she could never be talked into admitting the complete truth. One day she was playing in the front yard when a fox-terrier belonging to a neighbor darted at her playfully. With a shriek of fright, Susan fled to her mother and yelled:

"Mama, a great big lion ran down the street, jumped over the fence and almost ate me up."

"Susan," said her mother sternly, "aren't you ashamed of yourself. I was sitting here at the window and saw the whole thing. Now you go in your own room and get down on your knees and confess that it was just a little pet dog and you lied to your mother. Ask the Lord to forgive you for this sin."

Susan reluctantly went to her room and shut the door. In less than a minute she opened the door and poked her head out.

"It's all right, Mother," she said. "I told God all about it and He says He could hardly blame me. He thought it was a lion, too, when He first saw it."

CHILDREN HAVE an unconscious knack for saying things in a humorous way. All the timing and precious experience of professional comics are expressed innocently by the kids in response to ordinary situations. Here is a charming example:

Little Sammy had been invited to a picnic and looked forward to it for days. When the big moment finally arrived and he rushed off to the bus with his lunch under his arm, he could hardly talk for the excitement of it all. Then things began to happen. He got in a fight with another young man on the bus and had his nose punched. Then, at the picnic grounds, he sat on a bee with the expected consequences; he fell in the lake; a little girl stole his lunch; and he got badly sunburned.

Late in the afternoon, Sammy reached home in a disheveled condition, and as he limped into the living room, his father took one look at him and said:

"Well, son, it looks as if you had yourself quite a time at the picnic."

"Papa," said Sammy, "I'm so glad I'm back, I'm glad I went."

◆ ◆ ◆

Marjorie, aged four, marched into the drugstore to tell the news.

"We've got a new baby brother up at our house," she said.

"You don't tell me!" said the druggist. "Is he going to stay with you?"

"I guess so," said Marjorie. "He's got his things off."

◆ ◆ ◆

Little Ruthie ran into the house in a feverish state of excitement.

"Oh, mother!" she cried. "Our pussycat has got some kittens and I didn't even know she was married."

◆ ◆ ◆

Little Johnny came running into the house stuttering in his excitement.

"Mommy," he panted, "do you know Eddie Smith's neck?"

"Do I know what?" asked his mother.

"Do you know Eddie Smith's neck?"

"Well, I know Eddie Smith," answered the puzzled parent: "so I suppose I know his neck. Why?"

"Well," said Johnny, "he just now fell into the pool up to it."

"Well," said the friendly neighbor, "I hear you've got a little baby brother at your house. What do you think of him?"

"I don't like him," said Sally frankly. "He's got a funny red face and he cries all the time."

"Why don't you send him back where he came from?"

"Oh, I'm afraid we couldn't do that. We've used him two days already."

◆ ◆ ◆

And while we're on the subject of children and animals, I love this quickie:

"Hurry, Mother, and come look," said little James when he saw his first snake. "Here's a tail wagging without any dog on it."

MY FAVORITE Hollywood story concerns two little boys attending a private school in an exclusive section of the town where movie stars customarily live. The first youngster opened the conversation:

"I hear you have a new daddy."

"Yep," nodded the other.

"Well, I know you'll love him," seriously nodded the first. "We had him last year."

◆　◆　◆

A small boy came home from his first day at Sunday School and began to empty his pockets of money — nickels, dimes, quarters — while his parents gasped in surprise. Finally his mother said, "Where did you get all that money?"

"At Sunday School," replied the boy nonchalantly. "They have bowls of it."

◆　◆　◆

Another little chap was in church for the first time. When the choir, all in white surplices, entered, he whispered hoarsely, just loudly enough for the entire congregation to hear, "Oh, see, Daddy, they're all going to get a hair cut!"

◆　◆　◆

Ever notice the strange way a teen-ager borrows money from his mom? It goes something like this among the cool ones.

"Mom, will you loan me fifty cents? But just give me half of it. Then you'll owe me a quarter. And since I owe you a quarter, we'll be even. Huh, Mom?"

◆ ◆ ◆

I was questioning the kids one day about the games they liked to play indoors at home during the rainy season. They named a few of the standard games, and finally one youngster said he liked best to watch television. But another one snorted impatiently:

"I've been looking at television all my life. Why don't they invent something *new*?"

◆ ◆ ◆

The two little girls tiptoed into the living room and over to the sofa where their Daddy was stretched out for a post-supper nap. Wanting to know if he were *really* asleep or just pretending to be, the girls whispered and giggled as they stealthily approached. Finally, one of them darted forward, seized an eyelid between two little fingers and, lifting it up, leaned forward and stared at what was underneath. Then, sighing in satisfaction, she murmured: "Well, anyhow, he's still *in* there!"

◆ ◆ ◆

Who couldn't help feeling sorry for the disappointed little boy who sat in his garden crying his heart out? When a passerby stopped to inquire what the trouble was, the lad sobbed, "I've digged this nice big hole in the ground and I can't take it in my house."

◆ ◆ ◆

Who can ever forget the great game of "fooling the teacher" that we all learned to play at school? One young fellow was rather frank about it when his mother asked him, "What did you learn in school today, Clarence?"

"How to whisper without moving my lips."

◆ ◆ ◆

Bringing home the report card is another great indoor game in American homes. The object is to see how well a bad report can be presented, and how little penalty can be suffered for a bad mark. One duffer got an "A" on his presentation, even if his other grades weren't so satisfactory. Listen:

"Hey, Dad, you're sure a lucky parent."

"How's that?"

"You won't have to buy me a lot of new school books this next year. I'll still be in the same class. Ain't that swell?"

◆ ◆ ◆

And speaking of ingenious excuses, how about this one for the winner's circle: A very young ruffian was in the clutches of the law and he was busily framing his alibi to the frowning policeman: "I didn't really break the window. I was just cleaning my slingshot and it went off!"

◆ ◆ ◆

The little four year old cried bitterly when a large, friendly dog bounded up to him and licked his hands and face.

"What is it, darling?" cried his mother. "Did he bite you?"

"No," came the reply. "But he tasted me."

◆ ◆ ◆

You can always depend on a kid to speak his mind. In a barber shop the other day a six year old came in alone, climbed up on a vacant barber chair and piped: "Give me a haircut like my Dad's—with a hole on top."

◆ ◆ ◆

Mother was having her friends in for an afternoon of bridge. Suddenly, piping up through the buzz of conversation, came the strident tones of her five year old:

"Mama, I want to go to the toilet!"

Mother leaned over and reprimanded him: "Don't *say* toilet. . . . Whisper!"

The little one slunk off guiltily. But he remembered the admonition.

That night after the family had retired, the youngster tip-toed in from his room and pulled at his Dad's outstretched arm over the covers. Finally, Father mumbled sleepily: "Whatja want. . . ."

"I wanta whisper," urgently replied his son.

"Oh, all right. Then just whisper in Daddy's ear!"

Little Freddy had never seen a plate of Jello. He sat there at the dinner table staring at it for a long moment, watching it quiver.

"Go ahead and eat it," his mother ordered.

"Eat it!" the boy drew back in amazement. "It ain't *dead* yet."

The four year old, visiting the snake house at the zoo, wasn't a bit frightened or even worried by what he saw. "Oh, they're nothing but long tails with heads on them," he explained.

The little girl was making out a list of things she wanted for her birthday, when her mother

inquired what she wanted more than anything else.

"A baby brother."

"But, honey," her mother tried to explain, "you see, your Daddy and I would like to give you a little baby brother, but there isn't time before your birthday."

"Why don't you do like they do down at Daddy's factory when they want something in a hurry? Put more men on the job."

◆　◆　◆

There's nothing to compare with the sage comments of a three year old in pursuit of knowledge. Young Billy was lying in his bunk above his younger sister's bed. She yelled up at him:

"Whatcha doin' up there?"

"Readin'."

"Pass me down a book," commanded his sister.

"I've only got one," replied Billy, "but I'll be through in a minute."

Then he added thoughtfully, "If I'm goin' the right way."

◆　◆　◆

A four year old girl was carefully examining her playmate's toy car. She remarked about the glaring absence of a number of automotive essentials, and then became particularly upset when she saw the space reserved for the engine was empty.

"Don't worry about that," her friend reassured her. "If I put a little horse powder in there, it would *really* go!"

◆ ◆ ◆

And what about the conference behind the neighborhood grocery where the five year old told her gang about her mother's coming demise? She put it this way: "My mother'll probably die in a nervous wreck!"

◆ ◆ ◆

The boy was looking through the family album.

"Who's this fellow on the beach with you, Mama? This young guy with all the muscles and curly hair?"

"That's your father."

"*That's* my father? Then who's the old bald-headed, pot-bellied man who lives with us now?"

WANT MORE? All you have to do is listen. Just tune in on your neighbor's kids, or your own, and the law of averages is bound to reward you with all sorts of priceless gems. As I said 'way back at the beginning, there's a vast gulf between the world of children and our own. And every time we bridge that gulf—even if it's only for a moment—we recapture some of the freshness and spontaneity that make life worth living.